MEMORY LANE

Echoes of the Past

Reeta Dobriyal

Chennai • Bangalore

CLEVER FOX PUBLISHING
Chennai, India

Published by CLEVER FOX PUBLISHING 2023
Copyright © Reeta Dobriyal 2023

All Rights Reserved.
ISBN: 978-93-56485-05-1

This book has been published with all reasonable efforts taken to make the material error-free after the consent of the author. No part of this book shall be used, reproduced in any manner whatsoever without written permission from the author, except in the case of brief quotations embodied in critical articles and reviews.

The Author of this book is solely responsible and liable for its content including but not limited to the views, representations, descriptions, statements, information, opinions and references ["Content"]. The Content of this book shall not constitute or be construed or deemed to reflect the opinion or expression of the Publisher or Editor. Neither the Publisher nor Editor endorse or approve the Content of this book or guarantee the reliability, accuracy or completeness of the Content published herein and do not make any representations or warranties of any kind, express or implied, including but not limited to the implied warranties of merchantability, fitness for a particular purpose. The Publisher and Editor shall not be liable whatsoever for any errors, omissions, whether such errors or omissions result from negligence, accident, or any other cause or claims for loss or damages of any kind, including without limitation, indirect or consequential loss or damage arising out of use, inability to use, or about the reliability, accuracy or sufficiency of the information contained in this book.

Dedication

This book is lovingly dedicated to my dear father, Late Shri Swaymber Dutt Dobriyal. His life was an example of struggles and achievements. Though he is no longer with us, his presence continues to inspire and guide me.

He instilled in me the values of integrity, perseverance, and resilience, which have become the guiding principles of my life.

Through his own actions, my father showed me the power of hard work, fearlessness, love and compassion. He touched the lives of everyone he encountered with his warmth, generosity, and transparency. His ability to uplift those around him and make them feel valued was truly remarkable.

In the pages of this book, I seek to honour his memory by sharing stories that celebrate the resilience of the human spirit, the power of love, and the profound impact one life can have on countless others. It is my fervent hope that these stories will carry a fragment of his spirit and remind readers of the extraordinary capacity we all possess to make a difference in the lives of others.

To my father, whose love and guidance continue to shape my path, I offer my deepest gratitude. Your presence may no longer be physical, but your spirit lives on, illuminating my journey and reminding me to embrace each day with gratitude and a steadfast commitment in making a positive impact.

Finally, to the readers, I invite you to join me in celebrating the life of a remarkable man. May this book serve as a tribute to my father's legacy, a testament to the enduring power of love, and a reminder to cherish the precious moments we have with those we hold dear.

In loving memory of my beloved father, forever in my heart.

Contents

Acknowledgement .... *vi*
Preface .... *viii*

1. The Illusion 1
2. Silent Hopes – Ceylon 9
3. Lost Love 14
4. Behind Closed Doors 23
5. An Innocent Smile 41
6. A Tale Of Two Lives 44
7. Dompy 66
8. Laali 76
9. Beneath The Smile 80
10. Kittu 101
11. The Slithering Destiny 106
12. Alpviram 114
13. The Last Dream 117
14. My Scribble Voyage 126

About The Author *132*

Acknowledgement

I would like to begin by expressing my deepest gratitude to God for his guiding presence, a source of inspiration that has illuminated my path. I extend my deepest gratitude for the inspiration, wisdom, creativity, and perseverance that have been granted to me.

First and foremost, I want to thank my incredible supporter, my Spouse – Pushkar Sinha, whose patience, support, guidance, and expertise have been invaluable throughout this writing process. His belief in my abilities has inspired me throughout.

To my loving mother, Mrs. Basanti Dobriyal, whose unconditional support, understanding, constant encouragement, and belief in my dreams have sustained me during the highs and lows of this journey. I am truly grateful for her unwavering faith in me.

I am indebted to the dedicated individuals whose life experiences are penned in this book. Your willingness to share your experiences, expertise, and insights has enriched the content and added depth to my work. I am humbled by your generosity and grateful for the time you invested in helping me gather the necessary information.

Acknowledgement

I would also like to extend my heartfelt appreciation to the editors and publishing team at Clever Fox Publishing. Your expertise, meticulous attention to detail, and invaluable suggestions have transformed my manuscript into a polished and engaging book. I am grateful for your firm commitment to excellence and for believing in the potential of this book.

To everyone mentioned here and to those whose contributions may not have been specifically mentioned, I extend my sincere appreciation for your role in shaping this book. Each one of you has played a vital part in bringing this work to life.

Thank you from the bottom of my heart.

Sincerely,

Reeta

Preface

In the vast tapestry of human existence, countless stories are woven, each carrying its own unique blend of joy, sorrow, triumph, and resilience. In this collection of real-life experiences, I invite you to embark on a journey through these narratives that have touched my heart and stirred my soul.

These stories are not mere figments of imagination, but rather the echoes of real lives, real struggles, and real triumphs. They are the result of countless conversations, encounters, and moments of deep connection with individuals from all walks of life. It is through their willingness to share their stories that I found the inspiration to bring them to life on these pages.

Each story captures the complexities of human relationships, the resilience of the human spirit, and the profound impact of the choices we make. From tales of love and loss to redemption and hope, these stories offer glimpses into the kaleidoscope of the human experience.

While these stories are based on real-life events, I have taken creative liberties to ensure anonymity and protect the privacy of those whose stories are shared. Names, locations, and specific

Preface

details have been altered, yet the essence of their experiences remains intact. I intend to honor their stories while preserving the delicate balance between authenticity and respect.

Writing these stories has been both a humbling and transformative experience. They have allowed me to dig deep into the hearts and minds of the characters, navigate the intricate web of their emotions, and grapple with the questions and dilemmas they face. Through their stories, I have learned more about the resilience of the human spirit, the power of compassion, and the significance of empathy.

To the individuals who have entrusted me with their stories, I offer my deepest gratitude. Your willingness to open up, sharing your vulnerabilities & experiences has been an extraordinary gift. I hope that in bringing your stories to light, I have done justice to the richness and complexities of your lives.

It is my sincere hope that these stories will evoke your emotions and ignite reflections. May they serve as reminders of our shared humanity and the interconnectedness of our lives.

Within these pages, I invite you to explore the extraordinary within the ordinary, embrace the power of storytelling, and celebrate the beauty of the human spirit.

With heartfelt appreciation,

Reeta

THE ILLUSION

There are benefits of living in peri-urban areas where people are modernized, progressive and at the same time remain strongly connected to roots and follow beliefs. People living in peri-urban & rural areas are more aware of spiritual faith and its importance. Small-town folks are usually more religious and follow God in different forms as per their traditional beliefs. Even in the 21st century, in small towns and villages, we will find small temples in between farms, small red flags on Peepal (peepul or Bodhi) trees, small uniquely shaped stone covered with *roli* (red powder), *mauli* or *kalava* (threads) and flowers. These are different ways of praying, following, and observing the auspicious presence of God. Being a peri-urban kid, I have witnessed all these. I follow, believe, and respect this acquitted way of worship and beliefs.

In the northern parts of India, in small towns and villages, the concept of the dargah is prevalent across. Dargah means tomb of pir (or Peer, commonly known as Peer Babas' usually painted in white or sky-blue.

According to the stories I heard from old people of villages, these tombs were made in memory of Sufi souls or *fakeers* who lived alone, spent their life roaming around different places, preaching, doing noticeable work, and spiritually helping others. After their departure from the materialistic world, their disciples, and followers built small tombs for them in between their farms, sometimes near Peepal trees or beside roads in empty lands.

Nowadays, we rarely see *fakeers* or saints, but many people still follow the departed ones. In villages, it is strongly believed that these saints are the messengers of God and after their death, they stay close to God. So, visiting their tombs, praying, and offering them something as per your capacity will help in sending prayers to God.

I was nurtured in a religious and spiritual environment, and I have a strong belief in it. I was born and raised in a Hindu Brahmin family, but my parents were liberal enough not to stop me from following and visiting these tombs.

The story begins here………..

Those were the days when their were no mobile phones, internet, and social media. During hot summer days, we were forced by our parents to take power naps in the afternoon to avoid extensive heat outdoors. With a heavy heart, we used to stay inside home. But as soon as the parents' power nap turned into a relaxing sleep, we would make a way out to escape towards the playgrounds.

We would often engage in games of hide and seek, chor police (cops and robbers), or football under the scorching sun, leaving us drenched in sweat. The heat and physical exertion only added to the thrill and excitement of our playtime adventures.

One fine day, me along with two of my friends, escaped from this power nap and gathered outside a friend's home. It was a hot day of June month and there was nothing interesting to do in those harsh rays of the Sun. But, as we were already outside and had nothing to do, we decided to visit a tomb nearby. It was a Thursday which is considered an auspicious day to visit Peer Babas' *dargah*.

We decided to collect Rs. 2 (INR) per head to buy offerings and snacks. However, going back home to arrange this money was again a risky task. But our generation was raised in such an environment that taking such interesting risks was a regular adventure, unlike current days where kids sit in front of PlayStation and kill monsters in a virtual environment.

So, we went back home and in the next few minutes we all were ready with our share of money. We had to buy water & snacks as the visit had to be followed with a peaceful stay of one hour at an irrigation canal near the *dargah*, where we could sit, relax, and eat. We walked a few minutes to reach the nearest shop, which was unfortunately closed, so we were forced to walk another 10 minutes to reach the next shop. The long walk in rubber slippers, the humidity and the clothes drenched in sweat forced us to think whether venturing out in the hot afternoon instead of taking a power nap was actually a good idea. Though the body wanted to say yes, but our heart was not convinced to waste those precious time with friends, in sleeping.

We finally reached the next shop. The shopkeeper was happy to see unexpected customers at an odd time of the day. We purchased our required items and left for the tomb. We collected as many flowers as we could from houses which were on our way towards the tomb.

The three of us, gossiping and discussing important worldly affairs, filled with happiness, strolled along the deserted street, undeterred by the sweltering temperature of 40+ degree Celsius.

The tomb was in the middle of a large farm surrounded by plantations of wheat. To reach the tomb we had to cross the farm on a small trail of mud which was around half feet wide. The trail was narrow with wheat plantations on both sides. We crossed the trail in around 8-10 minutes, carefully and slowly with our tiny footsteps and finally reached the tomb.

The tomb was painted light blue in colour and was located just below a Peepal tree, with a boundary wall of around one feet height. Though we often visited the place, we felt a bit scared, probably because of the odd time we reached there. Once we crossed the small gate, we felt a sudden change in temperature probably because of the cool breeze of tree.

We noticed a small boy sitting at a corner of the boundary wall of the tomb. He was silently staring at the Peepal tree. Without any reason, our conscious mind stopped us from going near the young boy. We couldn't stand inside the gate and took a few steps back.

He turned his face towards us and smiled. His face was unfamiliar to us. It was a small locality and almost everyone knew each other. We were confused and had a strange feeling. He was too small to visit the tomb alone from any faraway place. He must be around 7-8 years of age which I could figure out from his appearance. The junior Sherlock Holmes inside me was not able to find anything further about the suspicious boy. So, I gave up and looked at my friends who were already out of the boundary wall, several steps away from me. I stared at them in anger for leaving me alone inside the gate in front of that little mystery.

'*Didi*, I finished praying. You can come and pray,' the boy's voice hooked my attention.

I tried to remain cool and replied, 'Yes, sure.' I asked him to continue praying if he wants.

He did not respond and began walking towards me or probably the gate which I was blocking. I quickly gave him space, he stared at me and smiled again.

'Why you are alone here at this odd time of the day?' I asked the boy. I immediately realized that I shouldn't ask this question to a stranger.

He gave me a look filled with a mix of slight anger, and confusion. I observed him struggling to comprehend the situation or find the right words to express his feelings. 'That applies to you three as well,' he replied.

On the other hand, both of my friends appeared furious and maddened by my question. It appeared that they wanted to eradicate my presence from their morning walk gang permanently.

As soon as he exited the gate, both of my friends swiftly entered, their expressions filled with disapproval. They began scolding me in hushed whispers, ensuring to keep their belongings on the ground as they prepared to commence their prayers.

Their intense emotions made it clear that my question had not been well-received.

Out of curiosity, one of my friends stepped out of the gate to check the direction in which the boy went. But her scream caught our attention and we rushed to her quickly.

To our surprise or shock, the boy was seen nowhere. We moved our head in all directions but there was no trace of him. We were in the middle of the farm and to reach the main road from any direction, it would take at least five minutes even if one walked at a fast pace. It was less than a minute and the boy had already disappeared.

We did not think these small wheat plants of a few inches can hide a three-four feet tall boy.

After a few moments of confusion and fear, we were sure that he is not around. Our bodies froze. We were stunned and stood where we were without moving for a few minutes. We looked at each other to figure out the situation and read each other's eyes. Without uttering a single word, we started running back with maximum strength.

After 20 minutes of running, which we probably did after our annual sports day in school a few months ago, we reached the staircase of our friend's house where we had met earlier and made the plan to visit the tomb.

We were still thinking if it was an illusion or daydreaming. After a long silence, we all realized that we even forget to pray and left all things at the tomb. But the scary feeling took over all other thoughts and we just decided neither to tell the incident to anyone nor to discuss it among ourselves. We silently left for our respective homes for the power nap. Sleep was far away from our eyes not only for that day but for many days and nights. On a lighter note, for months we willingly took those power naps without even being asked by our parents.

We stopped visiting the tomb alone without being accompanied by elders. But whenever we used to visit that place, our eyes used to search for that small boy. But he was never seen again.

Gradually that chapter got faded from our eyes and mind, but the mystery remained unsolved forever.

Life has driven forward at a rapid pace. As I have grown into an adult, I have attained a good education. Working in the different cultures, tech industry, cutting-edge technologies and traveling to Western countries. Despite these advancements, these intangible fantasies remind me of the wonder and magic that exist beyond the realm of logic and reason. A part of me still clings to illusions.

SILENT HOPES - CEYLON

I met this young boy in Galle, 125 Km south of Colombo, Sri Lanka. It was a sunny day and after a long walk at Galle Fort, I stepped inside a local market which was colourful and lively. I walked around several shops and finally reached a corner shop where a young boy was selling hand-painted magnets and toys.

The little, colourful shop caught my attention. Fascinated, I approached the boy managing the shop, drawn to him for reasons I couldn't quite explain. There was something unique about his character – a friendly nature, with a radiant charm on his face. It was a glow that spoke of genuine happiness, contentment, and a sense of dignity.

He started a conversation by asking me which country I belonged to while playing with my 2-year-old baby. He offered him a few toys. I told him that I have no interest in buying them and even warned him that my kid could break those toys.

But I was surprised when he replied, 'It is fine, madam. You don't have to buy them. Let him play here for some time, and if it breaks, I will fix them.'

His warm and welcoming attitude prompted me to engage in further conversation with him. Intrigued by his charm, I felt a natural inclination to delve deeper into his world and discover more about his story.

I learned that all mementoes and magnets were hand-painted by him. I picked up a few of them and observed them carefully. It was neat and clean painting on each of the products. All were beautiful, in different sizes ranging from 2 to 6 inches magnets, key rings and wall decors, depicting the beauty and heritage of Sri Lanka.

Having spent a significant 20 years alongside my sister, a natural-born painter with a profound passion for colors and canvas, I had acquired a perceptive eye for art and developed a keen ability to appreciate creativity and perfection. As I observed the boy's artwork, I couldn't help but was captivated by the clarity of his artistry and the harmonious combinations of colors he employed. Curious by his skill, I asked him if he had learned the technique of metal painting.

He replied, 'No, madam. Never in my life.'

I asked, 'Then how could you paint so beautifully?'

His answer was convincing and disturbing at the same time.

'I had a little liking towards colours. When I started painting, I perfected it quickly because of my "needs".

His last word "needs" pinched me and made me curious to know him more.

On that day I realized that our pursuit of perfection is driven more strongly by our needs rather than mere interests. This sense of truth radiated from his eyes.

He told me that he is pursuing his graduation in Literature at Colombo University. He hails from a small town named Hikkaduwa, down south. He attends his classes during weekdays in the morning hours and manages to find time to paint these magnets and toys during the evenings.

On weekends his routine is to come down to Galle to sell his self-made products in the open market. Galle, being a hub of tourism, is a potential market for him. His earnings depend on the flow of tourists. On some days he could earn a reasonable amount, on other days he couldn't. However, at the end of the month, somehow, he manages to arrange money for his college fees and to support his family.

After a quick conversation, he got busy playing with my baby and in between he was handling other customers as well. For him, it was a random chit-chat with a tourist customer but on the other side, I found this conversation deep and meaningful. A life of struggle and survival with dignity and still being happy and enjoying his time with a baby without thinking about loss or profit.

Ceylon (The old name of Sri Lanka) had a very tough and critical phase in the past. People not only lost their lives but their freedom, basic rights, peace, and happiness too.

Thousands have lost their parents, kids, husbands, wives, families, and friends. Their life was much disturbed for years. Though the past few years have been peaceful, the fear and pain could still be seen in the faces of people who were victims of destruction. However, people are working hard and trying to cope with their past and struggling in the present to make a better and stable future.

Ceylon is a neat and clean country with people who love nature and are aware of the importance of the environment. They have a warm and welcoming attitude toward tourists. Despite all odds and fear, life is still moving.

I concluded from my conversation with several locals & learned that they were emphasizing more on good education for their kids, which was definitely a progressive attitude.

Ceylon is a perfect example of 'Life Goes On'

This place added lively memories and a new story in the life of an avid traveller. This young boy requested to stay in touch on social media and asked to share with him his pics with my baby, which I clicked while they both were playing.

He offered an extra magnet to my baby as a token of love apart from the magnets and toys which I purchased not because of his need but for his perfection and my interest.

And I left the place with a silent wish for Ceylon.

LOST LOVE

Jai was a perfect man. He was handsome, had a charming personality, graduated from a reputed engineering college, and worked as an IT professional with a decent salary. He was always surrounded by friends and was good at heart. A person who can be relied upon and was always available for help. I knew him for more than 10 years and we had a very good equation as friends. We were so close that I often used to visit him and his family at his place.

Despite Jay's virtuous qualities, he faced dissatisfaction from two individuals—his parents. Whenever I visited his home, his parents would express their discontentment regarding his unmarried status. I didn't pay much attention to their complaints, as I believed all parents share the same concerns about their children.

Being the youngest member of the family, Jay was cherished by everyone due to his pleasing nature. However, his persistent refusal to get married without providing a concrete reason became a source of conflict within the family. Jays' parents longed to see him settled, hoping to alleviate their own responsibilities. Despite their tireless efforts to persuade him, Jay consistently rejected their pleas without explanation. While his siblings, an elder sister and brother, had given up trying to convince him, his parents remained determined to find a genuine reason behind his unwavering refusal. They were even open to the idea of inter-caste, inter-religion, or cross border marriages, considering Jay's previous experience working abroad. Unfortunately, all their endeavours proved futile, as Jay remained resolute in his decision.

One fine day I received a call from Jais' mother requesting me to visit them urgently but without telling Jai anything. I was perplexed.

But observing the criticality of the situation I took a half-day leave from the office to visit her. My mind was full of mixed thoughts during my ride. As I entered the house, I saw the old couple sitting on the couch silently. I was relieved to see them fit. They did not speak anything on my arrival. I rushed to the kitchen, gulped a glass of water, and then settled myself on the bean bag in front of them.

'What is this, Aunty? You scared me! Thank God you both are fine,' I said.

The old lady stared at me, and tears began to fall from her eyes. I suddenly realized my mischievous attitude. Feeling guilty, I quickly rushed to her side and apologized for my behaviour.

She placed her hand on my head and started sobbing. '*Beta*, it is fine, I am not angry with you. I am crying because of my destiny. You see, Jai is always busy in the office. His brother Vijay is settled in the USA with his family and his sister is also married and settled in Bangalore. We both are alone most of the time at home and we are fed up requesting Jai to get married so that we can relax and proceed for *theertha yatra* in peace. Jai is an ideal and lovable son. He takes care of us, but we want him to get settled now. He should have someone in his life. You all are settled and living your own life. Till when one can expect friends to support them? Everyone has their own priorities.'

Her every word reflected pain and worry. I listened to her calmly, sitting in front of her on the floor. I looked at uncle who was silently looking outside through the window, deeply worried about the future of his son. Then, I realized why aunty had called me there in Jai's absence. Jai and I were very good friends for so long that even our families were close. Jai was always with me through thick and thins. So, his parents wanted me to help them to convince Jai to get settled.

The task was really tough, but the plight of his old parents motivated me to support them. That day onwards I started my efforts to chase Jai and convince him for marriage.

One day, Jai and I were talking, sitting inside a café.

'What has happened to you? Why are you behaving like my parents?' Jai yelled at me. 'You are married, you stay happy in your life and please let me live peacefully.'

I couldn't stand this arrogant behaviour of Jai. I left the café crying.

For the next few days, we did not speak. I did not respond to his calls and messages. After a week, I found him in my office during lunch hour. He requested me to meet him in a café outside. I was still angry at him and did not want to meet him. But at the same time, his parents' request echoed in my ears, and I decided to follow him.

We went to a nearby café and sat at a table near the window. I ordered my coffee and started sipping silently. After a while, Jai interrupted and apologized for his behaviour. He asked me why I was after him regarding his marriage. So, I narrated the entire situation, explaining how worried his parents were. I scolded him for this pitiful attitude towards his parents.

He remained silent for a few minutes and after a deep breath, he began to open up. His face was filled with emotions and his eyes, with drops of tears. In a soft low voice, he started talking.

'I was in class 10th, and she was in class 9th. I met her for the first time in a school quiz competition where we were partners in the final round. I felt a connection with her in those couple of hours. We won the competition and had a little formal conversation after the award ceremony. After that day, my eyes used to search for her while I was at school – every morning during prayer time, every noon, and every evening after school. On every encounter, we used to smile at each other and exchange greetings. Days and weeks passed by.

One day, I did not see her at school. For the next 3 days too, I couldn't see her. I was getting curious about it. I don't know what made me so inquisitive that I went to her classroom and enquired about her. I learned that she had met with an accident and was admitted in a hospital. I felt bad and the whole night I was thinking about her.

Her face kept flashing in front of my eyes. With her fair complexion, chubby cheeks, big black eyes, and long curly hair, she possessed an irresistible beauty. Her name was Disha. Her attractive features and captivating charm left a lasting impression on me.

The next day, after school, I went to visit her in the hospital. As I entered her room, my heart sank at the sight before me. Disha appeared pale and her eyes reflected a deep sadness. Her vibrant energy seemed to have faded away.

She was surprised to see me. We talked for an hour and I couldn't contain my excitement. She acknowledged my visit and thanked me for visiting her. I was elated to hear that from her. She stared into my eyes to say bye, and something happened at that moment.

I left the place, leaving my heart with her. That was the beginning of our love story.

That was a time when mobile phones and the internet were a dream. We exchanged our landline numbers though it was not easy to talk. If her parents were not at home, she would call me and in case my parents pick up the phone she used to disconnect. In school, we hardly communicated with each other. We were afraid of our friends who might start pulling our legs if they saw us together. Once she told me how concerned she was about her bad scores in mathematics. So, I used to help her to study math during free time in the library.

Two years passed. We both were in deep love with each other. However, we never acknowledged it with one another but there was a strong bond and connection between us. The bond of love, care, and concern. We never missed a chance to talk over the phone and spend quality time together whenever possible.

One day, I requested her to have lunch with me in a restaurant the next day. We chose a restaurant which was a little distant from our place as we both were scared that someone would see us together.

She rode her bicycle, and I managed to get my father's scooter to impress her. I was in a white shirt and blue jeans, and she was in a pink top and black jeans. She was looking beautiful, as always.

Summoning all my courage during lunch, I mustered the words, 'Disha, I know it may seem too early, and we both are young, but I have a strong belief in my future success. Will you be my partner in this journey of life? I can't quite explain when or how it happened, but I've fallen deeply in love with you, and I can't imagine my life without you. Even if you choose to say no, I would never find anyone to replace you. Please take your time and make your decision freely.'

Her cheeks turned red, and she stared at her dessert plate. After a minute of silence, I touched her cold hand and added my apologies thinking that she did not like it.

But she interrupted me and said, 'Jai, I also feel the same for you. But I am scared that you will leave me.'

I said, 'I will never leave you even if you leave me.'

She smiled.

After expressing my feelings to Disha, my world changed. I immersed myself in romantic songs and eagerly waited for her calls on my landline. At night, I would lower the volume and engage in heartfelt conversations, savouring every moment spent with her.

She was in 11th standard when she asked me to help her prepare for engineering entrance exams. I was in 12th standard, busy preparing for my pre-board exams. I assured that I would help her once my pre-boards will be over.

My pre-board exams were to end on Saturday, and I asked her to meet me on Sunday in a bookshop. I was happy and excited about finishing the pre-board exams and, of course, meeting Disha.

Before leaving for the bookshop on Sunday morning, I found my father being furious and upset while reading the newspaper at the breakfast table. On a lighter note, I mockingly told him not to get worried about the whole world as we three siblings were enough to bother him. He did not smile at my joke and told me about the robbery and murder of a family in a posh colony. It was sad news. Those were the days when these incidents were very common & crime was at peak. My father instructed us to be more vigilant, to keep checking the landline if it is working and to make sure the doors are locked before sleeping.

After breakfast, I quickly rushed to the bookshop where I promised Disha to meet me. I picked few books for myself, and I shortlisted few books for her. Hours passed but Disha did not show up. I waited for more than two hours but she didn't come. With a heavy heart, I went back. I was worried about her health. At night I tried to call her, but nobody picked up the phone. Then I was sure that she is not well. I decide to visit her the next day.

I reached her house and saw an entirely different atmosphere there. There was chaos outside her house. I even saw few policemen standing there. I asked one old man what was happening.

He said, 'Didn't you know that the family in this house was robbed and murdered the day before? Those devils did not have mercy on even the kids. They killed both kids too.'

His words shattered me. I fell on the ground. A policeman called a few others and with their help, picked me up and took me to the nearby house. I was totally lost. I couldn't accept what was happening. I recalled my father telling me about the incident a day before. That moment devastated me and changed my life completely.

I remained lost for many days. I fell ill and got admitted in hospital. I couldn't attend my board exams that year. It took almost a year to recover physically but mentally I was still bearing the same pain. I had promised Disha that nobody can replace her and that I can't give that space to anyone else in my life. There is no point in playing with the sentiments of any other girl and betraying her.'

After he told this story, there was a grave silence. I did not know he has locked so much pain within himself. I was clueless about how to console him and even I was in shock hearing this throbbing story.

Jai stood up and left and I couldn't gather the courage to stop him.

There were three painful souls—Jai and his parents. I started walking towards my office, deep in aching thoughts that whom to console and how.

Staring at my computer screen without blinking my eyes for moments, I just prayed for Jai and Disha and requested God to reunite them in another world.

BEHIND CLOSED DOORS

It had been an hour since Neha was lying on the bed, staring at the ceiling. It was 9:30 PM, her usual sleeping time but she was still awake. She didn't knew the reason for her restlessness. It could be the new boring and dull ceiling, the uncomfortable and slightly stinky old bedsheet, or the clothes scattered around the room. Perhaps she was missing her family, who were miles away in another town.

Piya: Would you like to eat something?

Neha: I'm not hungry. Anyways, thanks for asking.

Piya: No problem. Go to sleep now, and don't cry. Goodnight.

Neha gives no answer, remains quiet.

Neha asks **herself,** *am I crying?*

A tear rolled down her cheek, which she had been trying to hold for long. She had been trying to pretend to be bold for sometime, but she failed.

That was her first day in that new apartment.

Neha had always lived with her family at her home, throughout her school and college life, enjoying a comfortable life with her own room and privacy. She was always surrounded with friends and family. However, when she found a job in the corporate sector, she decided to move to a different, unfamiliar city, far away from her home. After spending a week in the accommodation provided by her company, she moved to her new apartment that evening, which she was sharing with a girl she didn't knew and had never met before.

She had two reasons for choosing to share a flat with a stranger. The first was financial, and the second was the concern for safety and security in a new city.

That night, Neha discovered that she wouldn't have a good sleep as her roommate snored loudly disturbing her. It was 11:00 PM, and the pain was slowly turning into anger. However, Neha felt helpless. Lost in these thoughts, she finally managed to fall asleep.

She woke up at midnight when she felt something touching her body. She noticed that Piya was covering her with a blanket as she was shivering a bit in that cold night of October month. Being half-asleep, Neha smiled at her and went back to sleep.

The next morning, Neha woke up to an overwhelming amount of light and noise in the room. It was driving her crazy. The door leading to the balcony was open, the curtain was tied aside, the bathroom doors were open with flowing tap making disturbing noise, the kitchen door was also open & filled the room with odour of veggies & parathas.

Neha (to herself): Welcome to hell.

Piya: Hey! Good morning. As you still have to set up your kitchen stuff, I made breakfast for you as well. I thought you had to go to the office.

Neha: Ah, today is off day for me. I have a shift job. Thanks for the breakfast.

Piya: Oh, that's great. See you in the evening.

Neha: Yeah, sure. See you later.

Neha tried to convince herself that Piya was nice and caring, but there was something about her that she didn't find good. Neha was a highly organized person who never disturbed others, while Piya seemed careless, unorganized, and least bothered about others' attitudes.

Neha started her day with the usual routine, followed by some grocery shopping and, of course, buying a new bed sheet. By the end of the day, she finished setting up her room and arranging her things in the kitchen.

In the evening, she was talking on her phone in the balcony when Piya returned. After she finished her call, she went inside.

Neha: Hi, Piya.

Piya: Hi.

Neha: How was your day?

Piya: Good.

Piya went to take a shower. She came back and went straight to sleep without talking to Neha. The next day, Neha went to the office early and returned late, so they didn't got chance to see each other for the next couple of days as they had different work schedules. However, Neha observed that Piya would wake up in the middle of the night and talk to someone. Since they were sharing the same room, Neha unintentionally heard Piya's whispers. It seemed to be her boyfriend, and they seemed to have disagreements over various things whenever they spoke.

It wasn't like Neha was eavesdropping. She simply wanted to sleep, and she found it quite bothersome.

After a week, both had the same day off.

Neha: Hi, Piya! It's been a long time since I've seen you in daylight. (She chuckled)

Piya just smiled while lying in bed, deeply engaged in reading a book called *The Obsession: A Nightmare of a Past* by Nora Roberts. **Neha read the title aloud.**

Piya closed the book.

Piya: Yes, I like her books. She is my favourite author.

Neha: Oh, cool! So, any plans for the day? Shall we go somewhere, maybe watch a movie?

Piya: No, I don't like movies. I have some things to do, and then I want to finish reading this book. In the evening, I need to go out with a friend.

Neha: Boyfriend?

Piya didn't bother to reply and left to take a shower.

Initially, Neha thought they could be good friends, but as time passed, it seemed less likely. With each passing day, Piya became more reserved & distant. Sometimes she was rude and sometimes lost in her own world. Sometimes she used Neha's stuff without her permission, only to later deny it and argue. On other days she would apologize, saying she had taken it but had forgotten about it.

Neha was completely confused about how to handle the situation. Days passed, and she made few friends, focusing on spending time with them and ignoring the mess with Piya.

One day, Piya didn't return home after work. It was 10 PM. Although they rarely saw each other, they were still roommates and there was a sense of care for each other in that new city.

Neha called on Piyas' number multiple times but she didnt picked her phone. This made Neha worried about her safety.

After 10 minutes, she saw Piya's number flashing on her phone.

Neha: Hi, Piya! Where are you? I was worried, that's why I called.

Piya: I'm sorry, I was out with a friend, and my phone was on silent. That's why I missed your call.

Neha: No worries. I'm waiting for you. Stay safe and come home.

Piya: Actually, Neha, I will be staying with my friend tonight. I will come tomorrow.

Neha: Okay, that's fine. I'll see you tomorrow since I also have an off-day tomorrow.

Piya: Sure and thanks for calling. Take care.

She hung up.

There was a sense of relief, even though they weren't very close friends but was just a care for a flatmate.

The next day, Piya came home late in the morning. Neha spent the whole day on usual weekend activities like washing clothes and organizing things. In the evening, she noticed Piya making chocolates.

Neha: Wow, you make chocolates!

Piya: Yes, I love making chocolates. You can say it's my hobby. I learned it during my hostel days to overcome my depression... (she pauses)

Piya controlled her words and changed the topic. She asked Neha if she wanted to go out with her. Neha was surprised to hear that from her.

Neha: Yeah, sure! I'm going to visit my family next week, so I want to do some shopping.

Piya: Sure, let's go shopping, and we can have dinner outside.

Neha: Yes, sounds good.

Neha spent the whole evening shopping, and Piya observed her.

Piya curiously asked Neha why she was buying gifts for everyone.

Neha's explanation for buying gifts for her family didnt satisfy Piya & she continued to question her. Neha felt little agitated with this but chose not to indulge in any conversaton at the moment. She was composed & wanted to spend the evening with Piya. She didnt wanted any uncomfortable discussions which would spoil the evening.

Piya's continued commenting on Neha's gift purchases as she couldnt understand why she was buying too much. But Neha decided to be calm & hoped that with time Priya would gain better understanding of her perspectives & would also share her suggestions & thoughts in the matter.

Anyways , they both went to have dinner after shopping. Random conversations started & then took a turn towards their college lives. Neha shared her college experience, being a day-scholar she had limited fun & her college days were limited to studies & very occasional outings. She eagerly asked Piya if hostel life was more fun.

Piya: I don't know why people think hostels are fun. I swear I never had any fun. I stayed in a hostel, but it helped me utilize my time for my studies.

Neha was intrigued by Piya's response, sensing a deeper story behind her words. She decided to delve further into Piya's experiences, curious to understand her better.

Neha: Tell me more about your time in college, Piya. What made it different for you?

Piya hesitated for a moment contemplating whether to open up or not. Eventually, she decided to share her story with Neha.

Piya: Well, Neha, I attended one of the top universities in India, and I was the topper of my batch. It was an achievement, but it came with its own set of challenges. I had to work extremely hard to maintain my grades, and I rarely had time for anything else. While my classmates were enjoying college life, I was fully occupied in books and assignments.

Neha listened intently, realizing that Piya's dedication and academic success had come at a cost. She began to understand the sacrifices Piya had made.

Neha: I can imagine how challenging that must have been for you, Piya. Your hard work and achievements are truly remarkable. But tell me, How did you land a job in a reputed organization & I am sure they must be paying well.

Piya: After college, I joined this organization as an analyst. It's a demanding job, & yes It pays well. I guess my academic record helped me secure this position.

They continued their dinner, with these chitchats.

Later that night, as Neha settled into her thoughts, she couldn't help but notice the sound of Piya's voice, filled with distress, coming from the balcony. It was evident that Piya was having an emotional conversation on the phone.

Neha debated whether she should approach Piya and comfort her or give her some space to handle her emotions privately. However, when Piya's sobs became more pronounced, Neha's hesitation overtook her worry, and she decided not to interfere.

One evening, Piya came back early from the office, much excited. She told Neha that she is getting promoted soon.

Neha felt a rush of joy and pride for Piya when she heard the news. Seeing her friend excited about her career advancement brought a smile to Neha's face, and she couldn't help but hug Piya tightly, congratulating her wholeheartedly.

However, Neha's observant nature didn't let the tear in the corner of Piya's eye go unnoticed. It was clear that there was more to Piya's emotional state than just happiness. Neha paused for a moment, then she ignored it.

Neha: Let's prepare a meal to celebrate your promotion and our friendship.

Piya agreed and went to take a shower before joining Neha in the kitchen.

As Neha busied herself in the kitchen, her mind wandered back to the accomplishments of Piya. Am I feeling jealous?

Neha (to herself): No, no. I'm not jealous of anyone and she is my friend.

With a renewed sense of purpose, Neha focused on preparing the special dinner. She hoped that this gesture would remind Piya that she was valued and cherished, and their friendship will become better and stronger.

Neha's heart raced as she heard Piya's voice escalate into loud yelling during her phone conversation. The sudden intensity and Piya's defensive response caught Neha off guard, filling her with concern and fear. She instinctively abandoned her tasks in the kitchen and hurriedly made her way to the balcony where Piya was on her phone.

Piya was loud, '…visiting a psychiatrist doesn't mean you're insane. Seeking support and taking care of your mental well-being is a courageous and proactive step.'

She then threw her phone on the floor, which got scattered into pieces.

Piya went inside the room, switched off the lights, and curled up in bed, hiding under the blanket. Neha's assumption that Piya might be crying seemed plausible given the distressing phone call she had overheard.

Neha approached the bed cautiously and spoke softly, her voice filled with empathy and support.

Neha: Piya, are you okay? I heard you yelling on the phone. Is everything alright?

Piya remained silent. But when Neha asked her again, Piya had an outburst on her.

Piya: Stop being so nice and sympathetic to me and don't try to interfere in my world. Not everyone is having a perfect life as you have.

Piya's voice reverberated through the room as she directed her frustration towards Neha. The intensity of her words struck Neha, causing her to feel a mix of hurt and confusion. Piya's plea for Neha to stop trying to be empathetic and nice and to let her be in that situation, disturbed Neha deeply. Neha took a step back, recognizing the need to respect Piya's boundaries and honour her wishes.

Taking a deep breath, Neha composed herself and left from there.

Over the following days, Neha maintained a respectful distance, refraining from intruding on Piya's personal space. She shifted her focus towards her own plans and preparations, seeking solace in the anticipation of her upcoming visit to her family. Deep down, she hoped that Piya would find her own path towards healing. She had chosen to maintain a moderate level of distance from her.

As Neha embarked on her trip to be with her family, mixed emotions accompanied her. Sometimes she missed Piya's companionship and worried about her well-being, yet she understood the importance of giving her friend the freedom to work through her struggles independently. Sometimes she felt so negative being around Piya that she thought of changing her apartment.

Neha reached her home, she was greeted with open arms and warm smiles from her father, mother, and siblings. The familiar surroundings embraced her, filling her with comfort. She eagerly settled in, knowing that she had many stories to share with her mother about her experiences in the new job & place.

As the family gathered, Neha's excitement bubbled over, and she began narrating each moment she had experienced during her time away. She described her office, work, the places she had visited, new people she met, and the adventures she had embarked upon. Her words painted vivid pictures, capturing the essence of her journey, which made her mother feel like she had been a part of it all.

Neha's mother's eyes sparkled with joy as she absorbed every detail. The room was filled with an atmosphere of love and connection as Neha's family revelled in the joy of her homecoming and the stories that unfolded.

Neha's siblings chimed in with their own anecdotes and experiences, adding to the lively atmosphere of storytelling. The room echoed with laughter, hugs, and the shared bond of a family strengthened.

As Neha continued to narrate her adventures, she felt a deep sense of gratitude for the love and support that surrounded her. The warmth of her family's presence and their genuine interest in her stories reaffirmed the strong connection they shared.

With each story she told, Neha's heart overflowed with love, gratitude, and a profound appreciation for the moments she had experienced. As her mother listened intently, a smile danced upon her lips, reflecting the joy and pride she felt for her daughter.

In that moment, surrounded by the embrace of her loved ones, Neha realized how lucky she was.

She knew that no matter where her journeys took her, she would always have a place to return to—a place where her stories would be cherished, and her presence would be celebrated.

Neha shared the experiences she had during her time with Piya. Neha mentioned the strange behaviour and mood swings of her roommate. She expressed her concern and confusion about Piya's actions.

Neha's mother, being a wise and understanding woman, comforted her daughter and advised her to be patient and compassionate towards Piya. She suggested that sometimes people carry burdens or have personal struggles that are not apparent to others. Neha's mother encouraged her to be supportive and understanding, as it could make a significant difference in Piya's life.

Neha took her mother's advice in her heart and decided to approach Piya with more empathy and compassion when she returned from her vacation. She understood that sometimes people hide their pain and difficulties behind a facade, and it takes a kind heart to truly see beyond that.

Neha's gifts were received with great appreciation and delight from her family. Her home stay ended with blink of an eye.

After two weeks, Neha returned. Once she entered in the apartment. Piya was there to greet her with a smile, but Neha could sense the heaviness in her eyes. She decided to initiate a heartfelt conversation.

Neha: Piya, can we talk? I've noticed that you've been going through some tough times, and I want you to know that I'm here for you. I may not understand everything you're going through, but I want to support you.

Piya looked surprised, her guard slowly coming down. She hesitated for a moment before responding.

Piya: I... I didn't expect you to notice or care. I've been struggling with my mental health and personal issues. It's been a difficult journey.

Neha: Piya, I want you to know that I care about you as a friend. We all have our struggles, and it's important to have someone to lean on. I'm here to listen if you want to share.

Piya's eyes filled with tears as she felt the genuineness in Neha's words. She had been carrying her pain alone for so long that the offer of support felt overwhelming.

Piya: Thank you, Neha. I... I haven't had someone I could truly confide in for a long time. I've been dealing with anxiety and depression, and it's been a lonely battle.

Neha reached out and held Piya's hand, offering comfort and reassurance.

Neha: You don't have to face it alone anymore, Piya. We are friends, and friends support each other through the ups and downs. Let's navigate this journey together.

Neha observed that Piya had a collection of gifts among her belongings, and she noticed one partially unpacked suitcase.

Neha: Whom did you buy these gifts for?

Piya: Okay, so I did a lot of shopping for my niece, cousins, and younger brother. These are toys and books for them, already packed. For my aunt and uncle, I bought some clothes and haven't packed them yet. I wanted you to see them and tell me if you like them or not. If not, we can go and buy something else.

Neha: Yes, they're very nice. I like them. But I remember you saying that you don't like buying gifts for family.

Piya: Yes, I did mention it before, and I'm glad you remember. So, I have a chance to explain myself or correct myself. I used to think that way. But this is the first time I came out of isolation in the past few years. I tried to see things from your perspective and I found that your way of living and thinking is quite cheerful and brings you happiness. Even though you earn less than me, I see that you enjoy life more and worry less.

Neha: Hmm. And what about your parents? No gifts for them?

Piya was quiet for a moment. Neha was sure that this was the moment when Piya's mood may change, and she would start yelling or say something unexpected. But after a pause, Piya spoke.

Piya: Neha, I never shared this with anyone and only a few people know about it. You may have noticed that I have a boyfriend whom I talk to and argue with all the time. He thinks I'm insane, so I'm consulting a psychiatrist.

Neha was frozen. It was as if a serial killer was standing in front of her. She looked at the door, which was locked, and if she wanted to run, she would have to cross paths with Piya. Considering Piya's weight, which was at least 15 kilograms more than her own, there was no chance that Neha could overpower her.

Piya: Neha, what happened? Are you listening to me?

Neha: Yes, yes, I'm listening.

Piya: So, I think I need a psychiatrist to deal with my behavioural issues and anger. Hence, I'm consulting one.

She moved to the bed and laid down, staring at the fan. Then she turned to Neha and spoke.

Piya: My parents passed away when I was 8 years old.

Neha was completely shocked to hear this.

Piya: My father was a rich businessman. One day, he brought a new car, and we all were going for a trip. But on the highway, my father lost control of the vehicle, and the car collided with a heavy truck. That's all I remember. I woke up in a hospital after three days. I saw my uncle sobbing beside me. They were saying it was a miracle that my brother and I were alive. I asked about my parents, but they were just crying. After that, I never saw my parents. I don't even remember their faces. All I remember is what I see in pictures. My brother was so small that he was unaware of everything. My uncle and aunt adopted us. The business was gone, as we were both very small to understand anything. We stayed without our parents since childhood. For my brother, I was there, but for me, no one was there. I chose isolation and embraced books and studied hard. It gave me success in school, college, and at work. But I am broken from inside.

I met Mayank in college. He was my senior. I was attracted to him and we started liking each other. But because of my loneliness and depression, I have anger issues and some other behavioural issues. We are struggling in this relationship, though we want to be with each other.

When you came into this apartment, I was not happy. I didn't want to share my space. But yes, I wanted to split the rent, so I decided to share the apartment. But gradually, I started liking your behaviour and the way you live. When you talk about family, I feel like I want to have one of my own. When you went to visit your family, I felt the absence of a friend in my life. I cried a lot after so many years. I spoke to Mayank. After releasing the pain, I felt much better. After that I felt like meeting my family, my uncle, aunt, and cousins. So, I applied for leave and did some shopping for them, for the first time. I really want to thank you for all this.

Neha was speechless. She remembered now what her mother had suggested her. Though Piya was not crying and seemed relieved, Neha wanted to cry out loud. When she heard everything, she suddenly realized how lucky she was to have a family, and the jealousy she once felt towards Piya's job and salary disappeared. A sense of empathy welled up within her. She tried to control her tears, wanting to say so many things but unable to find the words. Piya looked at her and spoke.

Piya: Neha, I know what you're thinking. You know, earlier, I used to feel bad when someone tried to show me this kind of sympathy. So, I isolated myself. But now I realize the importance of friends in life, and that there should be people who feel both the good and the bad for you and who can share your pain. You don't need a psychiatrist. You need people who love you.

Tomorrow, I'm going to visit my uncle and aunt, and I'm so excited for the first time. Before, it used to feel like an obligation but not anymore. Tomorrow will be a new day, a fresh start. Thanks to you for being an inspiration of my fresh start.

They both laughed together and hugged. A few tears rolled down Piya's cheeks.

AN INNOCENT SMILE

We, the intellectual humans, are struggling every moment to keep up with the pace of fast-moving life. What we crave to achieve, we don't know.

We desire for achievements, yet we often find ourselves unsure of what exactly we are striving for. Happiness becomes a popular topic of discussion, with philosophies abound on how to embrace the unpredictability of life and find joy within it. However, many of us still feel disoriented, constantly tallying our desires and searching for fulfilment.

I do not claim to be a Guru or aiming to teach the art of happiness. Instead, I am on a personal journey of understanding, seeking to align my thoughts with those of others and determine if my approach towards life is heading in the right direction. I recognize that money holds its importance in our lives, but so does happiness. Striking a balance between the two becomes a delicate dance, as we navigate the complexities of our existence.

I wish to share a small story of a kid who changed my perspective about the real sense of happiness.

One October evening just before the Diwali festival, on a routine day, I encountered a life. A small market which is usually decorated during festive seasons. There, I encountered a little boy named Sonu, who had a flourishing business of *diya*s on the roadside of the market. He stocked around 200 *diya*s of different shapes and sizes. I inquired about his products and prices and was amazed by the way he replied. I sat next to him and asked if he goes to school. He said that he does in the morning, and in the afternoon, he starts helping his mother in making *diya*s. In the evening they would come to the market to sell them. A few more people asked him about *diya*s of bigger sizes. With alacrity, he said yes. However, the stock was with his mother who was sitting in the next lane, and it would take time to go there and fetch them. He looked sad. Who would take care of his shop if he goes to the next lane? There was a sadness as it would result in a loss of business. The sale would hardly allow a supper for him and not an iPhone, PSP, or any other gadgets of which he is not even aware of.

Then I interrupted. I told him that I can take care of his shop while he gets the big *diya*s for other customers. He looked at me in delight and told me the prices of all *diya*s in case any customer enquired. Then he ran towards the next lane.

A couple of customers came, bargained, a few bought *diya*s and a few window-shopped. Sonu returned with the big *diya*s with the hope of increased sales. When I handed over the money to him for the *diya*s I sold, he was excited.

He offered the diyas to me as well and said, "I will give you at discounted price"

I did not require those *diya*s but could not stop myself from buying diyas from him. Sonu smiled & I observed an innocent soul in him. I realised this is called happiness.

He was struggling each day, not for gadgets, not for movie tickets, not for branded clothes, but just to earn bread for his family, to pay his and his sibling's school fees, for his parent's medicines and to support LIFE.

A TALE OF TWO LIVES

A Tale Of Two Lives

Restless Amit, struggled to find comfort on his unfamiliar new bed. He compared the comfort with cozy embrace of his bed back at home. He coudnt sleep not only because of physical discomfort but also the home sickness.

He arrived Doha few hours ago only, following which he headed directly to his company accommodation.

Luxury had always been constant in Amit's life. He had grown up as a carefree and reckless young boy, indulging in a luxurious lifestyle, impulsive decisions and shortsighted choices.

Blessed as the sole heir of his affluent parents, Amit revelled in a life of fortune from an early age. Surrounded by boundless luxuries, he was accustomed to a lifestyle that many others could only dream of. However, this comfort had unintended consequences. It led him into the path of immaturity, irresponsibility as he became a rich brat which ultimately spoiled him & led to detriment of his own character.

On the other hand, Amits' behaviour was taking a toll on his father's patience. His father firmly told him that he should either find a direction of his life or else should leave the home.

It was now imperative for Amit to take some life changing decisions or else he would face unpleasant consequences.

Consumed with anger and frustration, Amit engaged in heated arguments with his father, desperately seeking support from his mother. However, she remained aligned with her husband. Amit thought to leave the house but was scared also as he knew his life will not be easy.

Anxiety and self-doubt agitated his mind. Where would he go? If he sought refuge at a friend's house, he feared they would ridicule him for his current predicament. The weight of these apprehensions kept him confined within the four walls of his room, isolating himself from the outside world. Days turned into weeks as he grappled with his emotions and the consequences of his actions.

Two weeks later, Amit's parents couldn't bear the situation any longer. They approached him, concerned about his well-being. His mother began gently, 'Amit, you're our only child, and we love you unconditionally. Since you were born, we wanted to give you everything. But somewhere along the way, we failed to notice how materialism is blurring your perception of what truly matters in life.'

She continued after a pause, her voice filled with love and worry, 'It's been a year since you completed your civil engineering degree, yet you haven't pursued any job opportunities. We're curious to know what's going on in your mind. We want to understand your aspirations and what path you want to carve for yourself.'

Amit found himself at a loss for words as his parents confronted him. The truth was, he hadn't given much thought to his future and ambitions. His mind was occupied with living in the present, relishing the freedom and joy of youth. He clung to the belief that this was the time to savour life, to pursue his desires without the burden of responsibilities.

In that moment, Amit struggled to articulate his perspective, for he had yet to fully grasp the long-term consequences of his choices. His primary concern was living life on his terms, revelling in the present without worrying about the uncertainties. The clash between his parents' concerns for his future and his own desire for unencumbered enjoyment created an impasse, leaving Amit searching for the right words to express his worldview.

Amit's father took charge of the conversation and posed a critical question. He asked Amit if he knew about the family's expenses, such as groceries, utility bills, loans, and their overall financial situation. He challenged Amit to consider how he would handle these responsibilities and care for his mother if something unfortunate happens to him. He asked this question so that Amit can confront the realities of adulthood and understand the importance of financial awareness.

Amit's initial response was to find his father's concerns amusing, thinking that his father had become old and insane. He dismissed his father's words as nonsense, showing a lack of willingness to consider the validity of his father's perspective.

Amit's father, determined to take action, informed him that he would no longer support him financially. He offered an opportunity for Amit to work as an intern in a friend's construction company in Doha(Qatar), with the possibility of a permanent position based on his performance. Amit had a week to decide, but regardless, he would have to leave the house the following week.

Perceiving the seriousness of his parents' actions, Amit realized that their change in behaviour was genuine. Aware of his own lack of initiative in finding a job, with some hesitation, he chose the path of interning at his father's friend's construction company.

With this decision, Amit was now mentally free. Instead of reflecting on the importance of his parents' support and the privileges he had enjoyed, he opted to spend his remaining week partying with friends, oblivious to the value of the time slipping away.

Amit failed to recognize the significance of his parents' sacrifices, the financial security they provided, and the opportunities he had taken for granted.

With a lack of enthusiasm, Amit prepared himself for the new journey that awaited him. While his mother was emotional, both Amit and his father seemed detached. Finally, the day arrived, and Amit embarked on his new path, oblivious to the twists and turns his future had for him.

First day at office, Amit had joined as intern. He was welcomed by his uncle whom he met for the first time. This introduction marked the beginning of Amit's professional journey, filled with uncertainties and potential opportunities.

Amit's uncle took the role of a guide, showed him around the office and introduced him with key people in office. He provided valuable insights into the city's rules and regulations, ensuring that Amit would have a smooth transition. Eventually, they reached Amit's designated cubicle, where he would begin his journey as an intern. Amit's uncle introduced him to Imran, who would serve as his mentor throughout his internship. Imran would be there to guide, support, and impart valuable knowledge required for the job role.

Amit's uncle delivered a surprising declaration, stating that their familial connection would no longer hold sway in their professional interactions. He emphasized that Amit needed to forge his own path, and for any assistance, Imran would be his sole point of contact, both in official and personal affairs. Furthermore, Amit would be sharing an apartment with Imran, solidifying the boundaries and expectations set for this new phase of life.

Amit was already emotionally drained out with recent events. It had left him indifferent and numb, making him less susceptible to further shocks & surprises.

Imran briefed him about his work profile and provided him with a list of tasks to accomplish. He explained that they would spend two days a week in the field, visiting different project sites. The majority of their work would be carried out from the office, with Fridays and Saturdays designated as their weekly off days. However, Imran emphasized that in critical situations or when needed, they might have to come on weekends.

As days passed, Amit struggled with his work and lacked focus. Despite Imran's efforts to help and guide him, Amit remained lethargic and unproductive in the workplace, causing issues and problems. However, outside work, Amit enjoyed being active and enjoyed whatever little luxury he could afford. Amit felt that Imran was a reserved roommate. Despite Amit's shortcomings, Imran consistently shielded him from the consequences of his actions.

One day, Amit's uncle learned about his behaviour and paid a visit to the office. He was agitated & scolded both Amit and Imran for covering up Amit's shortcomings. This confrontation left both Amit and Imran upset and disappointed. After work, they did not go to their apartment & planned to stop at the beach. They sat beside the sea, sipping tea in silence. Breaking the silence, Amit apologized to Imran for causing him to face his uncle's anger. Imran acknowledged his feelings, expressing his own anger and disappointment, not towards Amit's uncle, but towards Amit. Because of the fact that, as his boss, his actions were being questioned for the first time because of Amit's behaviour.

Amit laughed it off, dismissing the situation, and told Imran to take it easy, as it was no big deal. He then commented on Imran's supposedly boring life, stating that Imran had nothing to lose. Amit compared his own life to the one he had in India, expressing his frustration and disappointment with the current state.

During that moment, Imran reacted strongly to Amit's remark, emphasizing that Amit was fortunate to have born in a rich family. Imran made it clear that Amit had not earned his advantages, while Imran himself had experienced significant losses. Imran's annoyance grew, and he scolded Amit harshly, expressing his frustration and disappointment at Amit's lack of understanding and gratitude.

Amit felt sad & was feared too, realizing that he might lose the only friend he had made in the past three months. The truth was that since he arrived, he had distanced himself from his parents. Despite their attempts to reach out, Amit had stubbornly expressed his anger and resentment towards being sent away from home. He occasionally responded to his mother's messages on WhatsApp, but he relied on Imran as his only source of support and connection. Seeing Imran in this state, Amit was not ready to lose his last glimmer of hope and friendship.

Feeling remorseful, Amit apologized to Imran for his insensitive remarks. Imran remained silent, absorbing the apology. He then took the initiative to ease the tension by ordering two more cups of tea and some *samosas* from the nearby cafeteria situated at the corner of the beach. The gesture served as a small peace offering, allowing them to sit together, sip their tea, and enjoy the calming atmosphere as they contemplated the importance of their bond.

After a few moments of silence, Imran took the initiative to continue the conversation. He revealed that he was from Pakistan. However, Amit responded with a mocking tone, implying that Imran was boasting about his nationality as if he were from Russia or Israel.

Imran: Can't you be serious for a moment?

Amit (Laughing): I can, but after all that, you just say, 'I'm from Pakistan' as if I don't know. We've been together for three months. I already know where you are from. You've been living in Qatar for the past five years, while your family is back in Pakistan. I know all that.

Imran expressed his desire to Amit to take the conversation seriously.

Amit: Ok, I am quiet now.

Imran: Okay, that's what my passport says. My adoptive parents are from Pakistan, but my birth mother was from Turkey, and my father was from a city called Perth in Scotland.

Shocked to hear this unexpected revelation, Amit sensed a deeper level of seriousness in the conversation than he had initially assumed. He continued sipping his tea, but turned towards Imran, folding his legs, and wordlessly staring at him, his eyes reflecting a mix of curiosity and intrigue.

Imran: This story begins before my birth, back in 1983 when Doha was in its early stages of development. My father, Gary, was assigned here for special government services. However, by 1985, he had to retire due to health concerns. He then ventured into starting his own recruitment agency. Around the same time, one of his friends introduced him to a Muslim community group. Intrigued, Gary joined the group and became an active member. It was there that he crossed paths with my mother, Safiya, who owned a small event management company.

As Imran shared these details, Amit listened attentively, engrossed in the unfolding story and curious to know more about Imran's family background.

Days, weeks, and months passed, and as Gary's belief and interest in Islam deepened, his bond with Safiya grew stronger. They became close friends, supporting each other in their personal and professional lives.

However, Gary's business faced financial challenges, and it was Safiya who extended her hand by offering him a partnership in her event management company. Without hesitation, Gary sold off his business setup and joined Safiya as a partner, pooling their resources & started working together.

One day, Gary expressed his desire to marry Safiya. As an orphan & with no immediate family ties in Turkey, Safiya was touched by Gary's proposal but emphasized her unwavering commitment to her Islamic faith. Gary embraced Safiya's religion and expressed his intention to convert to Islam.

Gary became Ibrahim.

Safiya joyfully accepted Ibrahim (Gary)'s decision, and after completing the necessary rituals and ceremonies, they both got married marking a significant chapter in their journey together.

Ibrahim (Gary) and Safiya successfully expanded their business and began to enjoy a comfortable life. Their hard work paid off, and they were content with the progress they had made.

Then, in 1987, the couple received the wonderful news that they were expecting their first child. Overwhelmed with joy, they started envisioning a bright future for their growing family. Ibrahim made plans to visit his parents, eager to introduce his wife to them and complete the necessary formalities. With a mix of excitement and anticipation, Ibrahim left for his journey.

In the middle of July 1987, Safiya received devastating news – Ibrahim had tragically passed away in an unfortunate accident. The news shattered her world. With grief and despair, Safiya found herself contemplating the end of her own life. With no immediate family to lean on and now having lost her husband, she felt utterly alone.

However, there was a glimmer of hope that kept Safiya going— the life growing within her. It was her unborn baby that gave her the strength to continue her life. In memory of Ibrahim, she gathered all his belongings and created a memorial grave for him in the nearest cemetery, a place where she could pay her respect and cherish his memory. It was a solemn reminder of the love they shared and the life they had dreamed of building together.

However, the tragic fate seemed relentless. After giving birth to her baby boy, Imran, Safiya received another devastating blow. The doctor diagnosed her with stage three breast cancer. Safiya was shattered and felt like her world was crumbling around her. As she held Imran in her arms, she couldn't help but got reminded of his father, Ibrahim. The absence of Ibrahim weighed heavily in her heart, knowing that she would never see him again and that he wouldn't be there to witness their son's growth.

The news of her illness added to Safiya's anguish. She was worried about who would take care of Imran once she is gone, as she had no extended family to rely on. It was a difficult and uncertain time for Safiya, and she clung to her son, cherishing every moment she had with him, while also grappling with the fear of an uncertain future.

Safiya's worry about her son's future led her to make necessary legal arrangements for the benefit of her business to support Imran. She called upon her trusted supervisor, Ahmed, and his wife, Zoya, and revealed the truth about her deteriorating health. They were taken aback by the news and the weight of the responsibility that Safiya was entrusting them with.

Safiya humbly requested Ahmed and Zoya to adopt Imran, assuring them that his expenses would be covered by the profits from her business. After some hesitation, Ahmed and Zoya agreed, moved by the sight of little Imran, and understanding the gravity of the situation. Safiya shared her desire for them to raise Imran as a devout Muslim, ensuring he recites the entire Quran. She also expressed her wish for Imran to have the freedom to make his own decisions once he turns 18.

Tragically, Safiya passed away before Imran even celebrated his first birthday, leaving Ahmed and Zoya to fulfil their promise and raise Imran with love and care, following Safiya's wishes.

Imran joined his foster family and started living with them unknowing about his identity.

Imran was 7 years old when one day Ahmed and Zoya received a letter from Ibrahims' father (Imrans' grandfather) expressing his desire to see his grandson. It was a difficult decision. They pondered over the situation and considered what would be best for Imran. Eventually, they agreed to honour Ibrahim's father's request and decided to send Imran to Scotland to meet his paternal grandparents.

Till then, Imran was unaware of his true lineage and believed Ahmed and Zoya to be his parents. But now they revealed the truth and explained to him that he would be visiting his real grandparents in Scotland for a while, emphasizing the importance of family bonds. Imran was both excited and nervous about this new journey.

Arrangements were made for Imran's trip, and with a heavy heart, Ahmed and Zoya bid farewell to the young boy they had raised as their own child. Imran embarked on a journey to Scotland, eager to meet his grandfather and uncover the truth about his heritage.

Imran's experience in Scotland with his grandparents and cousins was challenging as a young boy. The cultural differences, unfamiliar surroundings, and the language barrier made it difficult for him to connect with them. Imran felt isolated and spent much of his time in crying, unable to adjust to his new environment.

Learning about Imran's distress, his grandparents and Imran reached a mutual understanding. They decided that it would be best for him to return to his foster family, where he had found love, care, and belongingness. Imran, now aware of his true heritage, made a firm decision not to go back to Scotland again.

Imran realized that his true family was the one he had grown up with, consisting of Ahmed, Zoya, and his siblings. Despite the revelation of his biological connection to his grandparents, he felt a stronger bond with his foster family. He found comfort and happiness in their presence and decided to continue his life with them, cherishing the love and support they had always provided.

As Imran paused, Amit was filled with mix of astonishment and realization. He had been living a life of privilege and abundance, never having faced any real challenges or experienced deep emotional connections. Listening to Imran's story, he recognized the stark contrast between their lives.

Amit's mind raced with thoughts as he reflected on his own existence. He realized that he had no stories to share, no real struggles or significant bonds with anyone. His life had been a series of superficial pleasures and fleeting moments of enjoyment. It suddenly dawned on him that he had been missing out the richness and depth that life had to offer.

Feeling a sense of emptiness and longing for something more meaningful, Amit was struck by the profound impact of Imran's story. It was like watching a thrilling and heartbreaking movie unfolding before his eyes.

Amit: What happened next? Please, Imran, tell me. It's such an interesting story.

Imran (laughs): You're still that curious and innocent boy, aren't you? Well, I appreciate your enthusiasm. It's just funny to see a boy who never lives in reality is interested in this real-life story. But hey, that's what makes you unique, my friend. Keep that curiosity alive. And yes I will continue my story some other day.

Amit: But Imran *bhai*

Imran (laughs): *Chal, aaj tujhe Pakistani biryani khilata hun!*

And they both left, engrossed in lively conversation, and shared laughter, walking together.

Next day was the weekend, and Amit managed to convince Imran to go for an outing. After Imran finished Friday prayers, they spent the entire day, having fun together. On Saturday, they decided to cook food together, watch a movie, and relax at home. It was a day filled with laughter and bonding between the two friends.

On Sunday, the first day of the week in Doha, Amit and Imran arrived at the office. Imran was pleasantly surprised to see that Amit was paying attention to all the instructions given to him and making an effort to complete the tasks. Despite the reports contained few errors, Imran was happy to see Amit taking the initiative and showing improvement. It was a positive change that brought a sense of satisfaction to both of them.

During the late evening, as they were wrapping up at the office, Imran received a call. His voice sounded joyful and excited. After he hung up the phone, his tears filled his eyes.

Amit (feeling concerned): What happened, Imran *bhai*? Is everything okay with your family?

Imran: I have become a father. My wife Rahat and I have been blessed with a baby girl.

Imran smiled through his tears and delivered the news.

Amit, though happy for Imran, couldn't fully grasp the emotions of crying and happiness intertwining. It felt strange to him. He remained quiet during the drive back home while Imran received numerous phone calls from friends and family, keeping him busy.

Once they arrived home, Imran ordered Amit's favorite food from an Indian restaurant, along with plenty of sweets to celebrate the joyous occasion.

After a while, Imran got free from phone calls and a video call after watching his newborn baby girl.

Amit (curiously): Can I ask you one question?

Imran: Yes, sure, ask me two, man. I can't tell you how happy I am.

Amit: I understand your happiness and joy, but why were you crying when you received the call?

Imran (chuckling): I wasn't crying, those were tears of joy. Some joys are so profound that they touch your soul and bring tears to your eyes. Becoming a parent is the greatest blessing in this world. It changes your perspective and makes you to do everything for your child, to give them all the happiness you couldn't have imagined. I will strive to provide my daughter with all the happiness in the world.

As Imran explained the depth of parenthood to Amit, it sparked a contemplation within Amit about his own parents and their love and sacrifices for him.

Amit's eyes filled with tears. It surprised him because he couldn't remember the last time he cried genuinely. He reflected on the moments he thought he had cried before, like when he fell from his bicycle when he was in grade 3 or when he desired a Play Station in class 5. He acknowledged that those cries were not genuine and were more of tantrums.

But today, as he shed some tears, he recognized the depth of his emotions and feelings for his parents. He acknowledged his own selfishness and realized that his past cries were just result of his kiddish behaviour. This time, his tears were genuine, a reflection of the deep emotions.

Amit rushed to the balcony and called his mom.

Mom (with tears): I've been waiting to hear your voice, my dear. I think about you every day and pray for your well-being. It's hard being away from you but knowing that you're safe gives me relief.

Amit (curious): Why are you crying, Mom?

Mother (voice trembling): I am not crying, Amit. These are tears of joy. I've been waiting for your call every night, hoping to hear your voice. It means the world to me.

Amit (apologetic): I'm sorry for not calling more often, Mom.

Mother (lovingly): No need to apologize, my dear. I understand you're busy. But your call means everything to me. I cherish our conversations.

Amit (promising): I'll make an effort to call more frequently, Mom. I miss you and dad too.

Mother (emotionally): Your dad is doing well. He often asks about you and sends his blessings. He wants to talk to you as well.

Amit (hesitant): Not right now, Mom. I need some time. But please tell him I'll call him soon.

With a heavy heart but a glimmer of hope, Amit ended the call.

Amit stood there on the balcony, trying to compose himself after the heartfelt conversation he had with his mother. He felt a mix of emotions—joy, a tinge of anger, and some hesitation. The prospect of talking to his father stirred up conflicting feelings within him.

Feeling a sense of relief and gratitude for the connection he shared with his mother, Amit returned to the room, where he found Imran sleeping in the living room couch after the hectic day and numerous phone calls.

That night, Amit found it difficult to sleep as the words of his parents and Imran echoed in his mind. The realization of his own shortcomings and the importance of genuine connections weighed heavily on him. The next morning, as Imran departed for Pakistan to see his newborn baby and wife, Amit felt he will be lonely.

However, instead of dwelling on his solitude, Amit decided to channel his energy into his work. He dedicated himself to his tasks, seeking to improve his understanding and skills. He actively engaged with his colleagues, seeking their guidance, and collaborating on projects. By immersing himself in his work and building relationships with others, Amit aimed to fill the void made by Imran's absence.

Imran returned to work after 15 days. Amit eagerly awaited his arrival, ready to welcome him back. When Imran entered the office, Amit greeted him with a warm hug and a firm handshake, expressing his joy of seeing his friend again. As they caught up, Imran couldn't help but notice the transformation that had taken place in Amit's performance & attitude during his absence.

Word had spread among their colleagues about Amit's remarkable work ethic and dedication in Imran's absence. Amit had been staying late, working on Saturdays, and even going on field trips to ensure the work was completed efficiently. The office environment felt different, and everyone noticed the change in Amit's attitude and commitment.

Imran was glad to see Amit's newfound enthusiasm and drive. He realized that his own story had touched something deep within Amit, sparking a sense of gratitude and motivation. Amit's realization of the importance of valuing relationships and giving his best effort had resulted in his remarkable transformation.

Imran felt proud of his friend's growth and the positive impact their conversations had made. It was a testament to the power of stories and the potential for personal change.

Later that night while driving back home Imran stopped the car at the beach.

Amit (surprisingly): Why the beach? It is not even a weekend.

Imran: *Chal chai peete hain, aur apni kahani bhi to puri karni hai.*

Amit smiled and ordered tea and samosas and carried their cups of tea as they walked towards the seashore. They found a peaceful spot to sit, with the waves gently crashing against the shore.

Amit: How's everything at home?

Imran: Everything is going well. (He shows Amit a picture of his daughter)

Amit: She's beautiful.

They were quiet for a few moments and then Imran continued his story which he left incomplete.

Imran: Once I returned to Doha, I didn't go back to school immediately. Following my mother's last wish, I joined a madrasa to recite the entire Quran. It took me a year to complete it. Afterwards, I resumed my education and rejoined school. However, after 3-4 years, my father retired, and we decided to move back to Pakistan.

In Pakistan, I continued my schooling and college education. During my early college years, I met a girl named Faiza. She happened to be a distant relative and frequently visited our home. My mother noticed my fondness for her and discussed the matter with my father as well as Faiza's family.

Initially, Faiza's family had concerns due to her health condition. They mentioned that she had a hole in her heart and would undergo surgery the following year. She was also undergoing medication. However, my family and I were not bothered by her medical condition, and we wholeheartedly agreed to the marriage. We followed our cultural traditions and had a registered marriage. Faiza, however, continued to stay at her house to focus on her education.

One afternoon, I received an urgent call from my mother, asking me to come home immediately. She couldn't provide any details over the phone. I rushed home and found everyone panicked. They informed me that Faiza's condition had worsened over the past two days, and the doctors recommended immediate surgery. The surgery was originally scheduled for a few months later, but due to the critical situation, it had to be performed right then.

I rushed to the hospital and managed to meet Faiza before her surgery. She was in a weak state and could barely speak. Her words before going into the operation room were heartfelt and selfless. She urged me not to put my life on hold for her, knowing that I had already faced significant losses in the past. Her words touched me deeply.

After that, I never saw Faiza again. She left this world, leaving me alone.

I felt that I was the chosen recipient of constant pain as if every person who was meant to be with me was taken away. The devastation was unbearable, and I found myself leaving home, aimlessly wandering for days. When I eventually returned, I abandoned my college studies and withdrew from social interactions entirely. It took me months to navigate through the depths of that despair and find the strength to move forward.

Despite the intervention of my parents and siblings, the pain and sorrow had enveloped me so deeply that it seemed almost impossible to shake off. It took me several months to gather myself and find stability once again.

Then one day, I decided to return to Doha. I visited the trust that my mother had established to secure funds from her business, which had been taken over by the board members. Initially, I was receiving a nominal amount of money each month. However, I was determined to reclaim what was rightfully mine. Through negotiations and the threat of legal action, I managed to obtain a fair amount of money from the trust.

With the funds in hand, I returned to my hometown, and I used the money to build a house for my parents, as well as to start a small business for my retired father. It was a way for me to repay their selfless love and support, and to alleviate some of their financial burdens. It brought me a sense of fulfilment, knowing that I was able to give back to those who had always been there for me. I resumed my final year of civil engineering studies.

After completing my studies, I returned to Doha and began working in my field. Over the years, I gained valuable experience and established a successful career. I was recognized for my hard work and dedication, and as a result, I received promotions and advancements in my job.

Two years ago, my parents insisted that I should get married again. At first, I was hesitant, as I had already gone through the pain of losing a loved one. However, I eventually agreed for the sake of my parents' happiness. I married Rahat, whom my mother had chosen for me. The rest of the story, you know. That's all.

Imran smiled.

A tear rolled down Amit's cheek as he tightly embraced Imran. Overwhelmed with emotions, he couldn't find the words to express his gratitude.

Tea and samosa were finished and so was this heart-rending story.

While returning Amit dialed his father's number but this time there was no anger or confusion. There was joy, happiness, and tears in his eyes. Tears of Joy.

DOMPY

Since childhood, I always had a special affection towards animals. While others saw them as pets, my love for animals was beyond. I felt genuine care and concern for these innocent creatures who couldn't speak for themselves. It was a connection based on empathy and a desire to protect and care for them. This love has shaped my values, taught me compassion, empathy, and the importance of advocating for those who cannot defend themselves. Animals have a way of touching our hearts and reminding us of a dependent ecosystem among all living beings.

As a child, I also longed for a pet, especially a dog. However, my parents were against my wish. When I was at a tender age of 12, I visited a friend's house and came across a litter of adorable puppies, born to their pet dog. Among them, there were six female puppies and one male puppy. Despite the male puppy already being reserved for adoption, I couldn't resist pleading my friend's mom to give it to me. Because of our close bonding, she couldn't refuse, even though my parents didn't approve. With great excitement, I brought the little cross Pomeranian puppy home, fulfilling my long - awaited dream of having a furry companion.

It had been almost 15 years since I brought that puppy home, and now I was working in Gurgaon and living far away from my family. I made it a point to call my mother every evening. It was important for both of us to assure safety in an unfamiliar city of Gurgaon (Now Gurugram). However, something was amiss during our conversation one day. My mother's voice sounded dull with low energy level. Concerned, I asked her what was wrong. Her response was heart-wrenching.

'Dompy passed away.'

I never expected that my mother will be so affected by the loss of a pet. In fact, she had always expressed her dislike for animals. But that day, her sobbing voice revealed an emotion that I had never seen before.

Overwhelmed by emotions, I ended the call with a heavy heart. Memories of my lovable dog Dompy flooded my mind as I made my way back to my apartment. Tears streamed down my eyes uncontrollably, reflecting the deep bond we shared. Dompy's sixth sense and unwavering presence in my life had left an irreplaceable void.

It was after much negotiation and persuasion that my parents finally agreed to let Dompy stay at home. However, they laid down a strict list of rules and regulations for him. While it was a compromise we had to make, we ensured that our home remained clean and orderly, and Dompy learns to respect certain boundaries.

Within my mind, I knew that I just had to click 'I agree' to all the terms and conditions even without reading it. As my only wish was to get approval to get Dompy at home.

I recall how my father would often discourage me from keeping Dompy, emotionally manipulating me by making me feel guilty for separating him from his family. He would suggest that it wasn't fair to the animal and I should send him back. Those conversations would deeply affect me, and I would start shedding tears, contemplating whether it was the right decision. However, my siblings were quick to recognize my father's tactics and assured me that he was simply playing on my emotions because he didn't want any pets.

The memories of my adorable dog Dompy remain vivid in my mind. Like a pristine bundle of white snow, he was incredibly soft and cute. However, there were funny and sometimes frustrating situations in his puppyhood – he seemed to resist growing for the first 5-6 months. His extremely small size made it challenging for us to protect him from birds and cats, and it was amusing also, that he couldn't bark yet. He resembled a fluffy toy, bringing joy and laughter in our lives.

I remember how my brother and sister would go to great lengths to make Dompy bark. They would come up with all sorts of tricks and pranks, determined to elicit even the smallest bark from him. Whether it was to scare him at night by switching off all the lights and hiding or turning on the tap of the washbasin to create loud noises, they were relentless in their efforts. I found it amusing, but they were fully dedicated to their mission to make Dompy bark.

At first, my mother kept distance from Dompy, not really comfortable with him around. However, as our school days progressed, she was left with no choice but to take him to the garden for his nature call breaks and walks. Dompy, in his playful nature, would often annoy her by chewing her slippers or being mischievous. Yet, he would look at her with his small, red eyes and wag his tail, showering her with his affection. He would even lick her legs, trying to show his love for her. Although my mother would wash her hands and feet multiple times after touching him, it was evident that Dompy's charm had started to win her over.

Dompy had become an indispensable member of our family. He had a discerning nature when it came to liking people. Apart from our immediate family, he had a special fondness for our driver,

Uncle Ramdas, and a selected few individuals. Dompy never allowed anyone else to touch him.

I recall an incident when he accidentally banged the door while playing with me, resulting in a wound on his cheek. Despite the pain, he tried to conceal his injury, displaying his resilient and stoic nature.

Three days after the incident, we observed that the wound on Dompy's cheek had developed infection, and he had difficulty in eating. His eyes were filled with tears, indicating his pain and discomfort. Despite our attempts to get him into the car, he resisted and found a hiding spot. It was our trusted driver, Uncle Ramdas, who took charge of the situation. He skillfully convinced Dompy to sit on his bicycle and rushed him to the veterinarian. Dompy underwent surgery, but unfortunately, the dog chain securing him was accidentally opened, allowing him to escape the hospital premises.

Ramdas uncle arrived home, panicking. With his voice trembling, he said, 'Babu, Dompy ran away. What should we do?'.

But instead of getting worried, I burst into laughter. Uncle was taken aback, thinking that I had lost my mind. Later I told him, that I was laughing because Dompy had managed to escape from the hospital and had found his way back home. This brought some relief to Uncle Ramdas.

The incident of Dompy's wound had three significant impacts. Firstly, it brought my mother closer to him as she took charge of ensuring that he ate despite his condition. Dompy, in turn, developed a special bond with her. Secondly, the wound left a permanent scar on his cheek, a reminder of his adventurous escape from the hospital. And lastly, during this time, he discovered his taste for pastries, which proved to be a challenge for us to resist his pleading eyes whenever we indulged in these treats.

Now, it became a weekly routine for Dompy to demand pastries, refusing to eat his regular food until he got his desired treat. He would sit outside the kitchen, fixating his beautiful, teary eyes on my mother, silently pleading for a pastry. My mother would then turn to us, requesting someone to bring a pastry for Dompy as he refused to eat without it. This entire situation would often infuriate my father, but it never failed to make me laugh, witnessing Dompy's persistence and my mother's connection with him.

Despite his moderate height, Dompy had the remarkable ability to jump over a 4-feet boundary wall. So, he no more needed chain or assistance if he wished to go out. He could manage it himself. Taking advantage of his agility and independence which allowed him to roam freely, he used to visit a neighbour regularly.

Breaking their flowerpots, peeing in their veranda, and then asking for food became a routine for Dompy. He was becoming mischievous day by day. Sometimes, he even showed his dislike towards their guests, and despite these antics, he managed to charm his way into their hearts.

Later, this neighbour family moved out of the home, and coincidentally, a veterinary doctor moved in, making it convenient for Dompy's vaccinations and minor health concerns. However, as soon as Dompy discovered the new occupant, he stopped visiting the house altogether, creating a humorous situation for us.

Dompy had a unique habit of joining the family for dinner at the same time. Every evening, he would stand by the terrace door, patiently waiting for someone to open it. After a playful session of running and jumping around, he would then bang his heads and leg on the door, or scratch the door with his paws, signalling that it was time for him to come down. Once he comes downstairs, he would first come to my father and than to us to check if we had finished our dinner. If, by chance, we had finished our dinner before him, he would give my mother a sad look and either hide under the couch or sit on his chair, turning his back towards us. No matter what we tried, he wouldn't eat his food being upset that we finished our food before him. It was his unique way of showing his preference for eating together as a family and showing anger when that preference was not considered.

During summer, Dompy had a peculiar habit of drinking chilled water straight from the refrigerator. Sometimes, he would even demand ice cubes to play with. In contrast, during the winter season, he would always insist on having warm water. These habits of his always annoyed my father and my Nani, who used to visit us sometimes.

She often questioned why we didn't get a cow instead, as it would provide milk & a better deal than a mischievous dog. I always used to laugh on her innocence & her dislike towards Dompy. But She was too sweet & used to love me to the moon.

I was not sure if Dompy liked or disliked my Nani, but he definitely respected her. He understood that she does not like dogs, so he never approached her or touched her belongings. During her meals, he would keep his distance, and if she was out for an evening walk, he would quietly change his path to avoid any interaction. He sensed her boundaries & chose to give her space.

With our interest in planting, me & my mother did quite a effort into nurturing a beautiful gerbera flower in our garden, but Dompy seemed to have some personal grudges with that flower plant. Whenever he noticed the new bud grown, he would bite the bud and throw it at the door. After his mischievous act, he would disappear for hours, knowing very well that he would be scolded for his behaviour.

When Kittu, the Kitten, joined our family, an interesting dynamic unfolded between Dompy and my father. Both of them shared a mutual dislike for Kittu's presence in our home.

Once, a reckless driver collided with Dompy, leaving us all feeling helpless and devastated. Despite our efforts and multiple visits to the doctor, his condition remained critical, and we began to lose hope. However, my mother, always the eternal optimist and fiercely devoted to those she loves, went extra mile to take care of him. Through her unwavering dedication, Dompy miraculously pulled through and survived. It was a testament of the power of love and the resilience of life. Dompy continued to be a cherished part of our family for a remarkable 15 years, filling our lives with happiness, mischief, and unwavering loyalty.

Throughout Dompy's life, One mystery remained unfolded that puzzled us, he would never eat food on Tuesdays. We would think that Dompy has innate sense of the day & may be fasting on these days. Which is surely not accepted from any animal. We couldn't help but wonder how he knew.

During his last years, as Dompy grew older, he remained less enthusiastic and less active, he started spending most of his time in his designated room. Whenever he comes out, he would seek the comforting presence of my mother. In the evenings, he would join my father, watching TV together as if enjoying their shared moments.

As he aged, Dompy's appetite also reduced, and to our surprise, he completely stopped chewing on my gerbera plants. He was intelligent & he knew that those plants were close to me & thus he showed respect by not chewing them anymore.

The night when I heard news of Dompy's demise was sombre for me, filled with a deep sadness. I couldn't help but was wondering about the circumstances surrounding Dompy's passing. I called my mother the next day, knowing that she would be feeling better. She shared the details with me, recounting how after lunch, she had opened the gates for Dompy to enjoy his freedom. Being old, he couldn't jump anymore, and he cherished his solitary walks without any chains. On his last day, after a short walk of 5-8 minutes, he returned, trembling. Sensing something was wrong, my mother tried to comfort him, offered him water. He drank the water and looked at her with his teary eyes as if he was bidding his farewell. Then sadly, he peacefully passed away.

As, I was listening to my mother, I could not control my emotions. She continued, telling me that he was buried in our orchard, which lay in our backyard. I could only manage to ask my mother to plant some gerbera flowers on his grave. We shared a moment of silence before hanging up the call.

To our astonishment, despite our utmost endeavors, the gerbera flowers gradually wilted away, failing to establish a flourishing presence in my home following the heartening departure of Dompy.

There are many interesting stories & incidences with Dompy that remain etched in my memory. Whether I stroll through the garden, savouring a pastry, reminiscing about my late father, or when my kids inquire about having a pet, these memories resurface, and I find solace in sharing them with others. Dompy's presence in our lives left an indelible mark, and his stories continue to bring joy, laughter, and nostaglia to those who hear them.

LAALI

It was a hectic day. I had to cover three long-route cities including Indore, Ujjain, and Omkareshwar in a single day, starting from Delhi, with my best companion, my mother.

However, the day was passing by and after visiting the holy temple of Omkareshwar, we wanted to relax and restore energy before we could proceed further to our next destination.

Feeling hungry, we walked down the road and discovered a small *dhaba* (roadside restaurant) nearby. It was a sweet little place serving tea, coffee, cold drinks, and mouth-watering snacks. We grabbed our chairs, adjusted ourselves and filled our stomachs. We were tired but mentally relaxed as our journey was almost successful after visiting Mahakaleshwar and Omkareshwar.

Indore was our last halt, after which the next day we had to proceed back home. While having tea, I saw a small girl standing in front of me, smiling. At first, I thought she is demanding something. Looking at her innocent gesture, I approached her and held her hands. She wasn't scared and continued smiling. I asked her name, and she replied in a sweet voice, 'Laali.'

A four-year-old dusky girl, quite confident, fearless, and cheerful.

The old man serving us tea and snacks told us that Laali was his granddaughter. Then he pointed to a lady wearing a shabby saree who was making tea inside the *dhaba*. She was his daughter-in-law. When she saw me looking at her, she also smiled at me. I was delighted with their innocent gestures and welcoming nature. I offered some snacks to the little girl, and she happily accepted my offer. But her grandfather stopped her saying that it is for *didi* (me).

He got a bit agitated and reminded her not to take anything from customers and suggested asking her mother for any requirements.

Laali turned to me and smiled again. What an innocent and pure act! I asked Laali if she would come with me to Delhi for which she nodded her head in yes. Her mother and grandfather started laughing loudly. I told Laali, who was now sitting on my lap, that I will be sending her to school.

Her grandfather replied, we are already sending Laali to school.

After that, the poor old man told his story in short. 'We are poor, my son works in a factory and my daughter-in-law helps me in the *dhaba*. But we are earning enough to send her to school. We will educate her and make her "Memsaab", like you.'

His words warmed my heart. While working at the roadside stall and observing girls like me, he had a dream in his eyes of seeing his granddaughter becoming a "Memsaab."

I had never experienced the presence of a grandfather in my own life and the incident stirred profound emotions within me. I was deeply moved by the love and care shown by a poor grandfather for his granddaughter.

In today's world, where society forces the kids to beg and the issue of the alarming prevalence of girl feticide remains evident in various regions, this family has such a positive thought. They were working hard and living with dignity. They were nurturing the kid with so much positivity and good manners. I was amazed. I stayed there for a couple of minutes and listened to what the old man said. While returning, I offered Laali a few candies, as a token of love. This time, she looked at her grandfather who permitted her to accept them. She smiled, took all the candies, and waved me goodbye.

I felt a connection with Laali in that little span of time. It looked like I had a strong bond and relationship with her. I left unwillingly from there with a hope to visit the place again and see Laali changed, a grown-up girl going to school and chasing the dreams of her family. This incident is very close to my heart, and it changed my perception completely. I appreciate the thought of Laali's grandfather. If the rest of us too had such positive thoughts, our country will be different and more beautiful.

Be the change. Spread happiness always…

BENEATH THE SMILE

Jaya is sitting alone in the room, feeling nervous and anxious. She can hear laughter and murmurs from outside, accompanied by folk songs playing on the stereo system. Exhaustion, nervousness, and excitement—all swirled within her at the same time.

Jaya got married just yesterday. After the emotional farewell ceremony, known as *Vidai*, she arrived at her new home in the middle of the night. After a few hours of broken sleep, she was woken up by her sister-in-law to get ready for the traditional *muh dikhai* ritual. Her sister-in-law helped her to get ready and instructed her to wait in this room. It has been 30 minutes since her sister-in-law left, and there has been no sign of Hitesh, her husband. Jaya couldn't help but wonder why he hasn't come to check on her or see if she needs anything. After all, he is her husband, and a simple gesture of concern would mean a lot to her.

Being lost in her thoughts, Jaya was startled when her mother-in-law, Snehlata Shah, entered the room.

Snehlata: Jaya, are you ready?

Jaya: Mummy Ji, Yes. Nisha helped me.

Snehlata: helped you? By dressing you in such a plain saree? This is not acceptable. We must uphold the respect of the Shah family. Nisha, go and find a nice, heavy saree from my room. Make sure it's not from Jaya's belongings. Her parents have given her cheap things. (She called Nisha loudly.)

Nisha: But, Mom, it's just a saree. Does it really matter?

Snehlata: Of course, it matters! Presentation is everything. Now, go and get a suitable saree immediately.

Jaya was taken aback by her mother-in-law's words. She couldn't believe that her parents' efforts in selecting the best things for her wedding were disregarded as cheap. She remembered her mother-in-law's words before marriage about not demanding anything and considering her a valuable addition to their family.

Jaya felt a mix of embarrassment and sadness. She wished that her mother-in-law will give her same love & support as she got from her parents. She remains silent, trying to keep her composure and not letting the comments affect her on this special day.

Nisha's gesture and offer of support provided a glimmer of hope and comfort amidst the challenging situation. Grateful for Nisha's intervention, Jaya nodded and followed her, hoping for a moment of solace and understanding, away from the judgmental atmosphere in the room.

Nisha: *Bhabhi*, I understand you're upset about what Mom said, but please ignore her. She tends to get panicked when she has to handle household matters. But she is a good person at heart.

Jaya: (reflecting) Cheap things? My father has a garments business, and he chose the best for me for my wedding. How could she say that?

Nisha: (grabbing Jaya's hand) Bhabhi, let's go. I will help change your outfit.

Jaya: Nisha, do you know where Hitesh is? I haven't seen him since I arrived.

Nisha: Yes, Bhabhi. He's exhausted from all the wedding rituals. So, he's sleeping in the guest room with his friends. I told him to wake up and get ready for the rituals.

Jaya: (murmuring) Still, he could have come to check on me at least once.

Nisha: (smiling) He asked me multiple times to take care of you and make sure you have everything you need. He wanted to come last night to see if you were settled, but mom didn't allow it because of some traditions and rituals, you know.

Jaya: (forcing a smile) I guess that makes sense. Anyways, I was just expecting him to check on me, but I understand.

Nisha's reassurance and explanation helped ease Jaya's anger and frustration. She found Nisha an understanding and empathetic person, despite her mother-in-law's behaviour. She tried to convince herself that Hitesh's absence was due to circumstances beyond his control. Despite her efforts, some uneasiness still lingered within her, but she chose to put on a brave face and smiled, accepting the situation for now.

In the late evening, as the ceremony was completed, Snehlata was seen bustling around, bidding farewell to the guests while using every opportunity to boast about her family and son.

Jaya: Nisha, It was a very exhausting day. Thank you for being there with me throughout the ceremony. I appreciate your support.

Nisha: Don't mention it, Bhabhi. I know it can be overwhelming, but I'm here for you. Are you hungry? Let me get you something to eat.

Jaya: Yes, I'm famished. Just some light snacks would be fine.

Nisha quickly brings some snacks and water for jaya & she started eating.

Jaya: (sighs) I never imagined that the wedding would be so grand and extravagant. All these expensive gifts and ornaments, it's overwhelming.

Nisha: I understand, Bhabhi. Our family likes to show off sometimes. But remember, it's just material possessions. What truly matters is your happiness and well-being.

Jaya: You're right, Nisha. I've always valued my independence and education. It's just hard to hear all these talks about wealth and status. I hope I can find a balance between my aspirations and the expectations placed on me.

Nisha: I believe in you, Bhabhi. You're smart and capable. Don't let these external pressures define your worth. Take your time to figure out your career and pursue your dreams.

Jaya: Thank you, Nisha. Your words mean a lot to me. I'm grateful to have you as my sister-in-law.

They share a warm smile as Jaya continues to eat, feeling more comfortable in Nisha's presence.

Snehlata instructed Jaya to join her in the kitchen and prepare dinner, citing it as a customary part of the post-wedding rituals. Despite Jaya's exhaustion since days of wedding preparations and ceremonies, she couldn't bring herself to voice her weariness and complied silently.

As the guests left the home, Jaya stepped into the kitchen and noticed an elderly woman sitting in the corner, enjoying a cup of tea. The woman, introducing herself as Dulari, revealed that she had been working in the house for the past 40 years. She witnessed the birth of Hitesh and Nisha. Affectionately known as Kaki by everyone, she extended a warm welcome to Jaya, the newlywed bride.

While Jaya was engrossed in listening to Dulari, Hitesh and Nisha entered the kitchen.

Kaki: Baba, Snehlata Didi said that the new daughter-in-law will cook dinner today.

Hitesh: No, Kaki, she doesn't have to cook today.

Kaki: But Baba, Snehlata Didi said that it's a ritual.

Hitesh: No, Kaki, she doesn't even know her way around the kitchen or anyone's taste. Besides, she had a tiring week. You start cooking, and Nisha will help you. I'll talk to mom. The ritual can be performed tomorrow.

Jaya felt relieved and gratitude upon hearing Hitesh's words. She realized that he cared for her well-being and didn't want her to bear the additional responsibility of cooking after a tiring week.

Finally, Jaya reached her room, feeling exhausted from the day's events. She sighed with relief, hoping for a moment of tranquillity. During dinner, she noticed that her mother-in-law, Snehalata, was not present at the dinner table. With Curiosity, she approached Nisha to inquire about her absence.

Jaya: Nisha, where is mummy Ji? I didn't see her at dinner.

Nisha: Oh, she is tired. She said she'll have dinner in her room tonight. She must be resting.

Jaya nodded, understanding that the day had taken a toll on her mother-in-law. However, her attention was drawn to the presence of her father-in-law, Mr. Shah, who was sitting at the dining table. This was only the third time Jaya had seen him. The first was during the initial meeting to discuss the marriage, and the second was during the wedding ceremonies. On all these occasions, he seemed to appear and disappear, remaining a mysterious figure in her mind. As she observed him closely, she noted his average height, slightly overweight physique, and fair complexion. His face displayed a lack of expression, making it difficult for Jaya to gauge his thoughts and emotions.

Being lost in her thoughts, Jaya was suddenly startled by Mr. Shah's deep voice, bringing her attention back to the present.

Mr. Shah: Jaya, I hope you're adjusting well. If there's anything you need, don't hesitate to ask.

Jaya: Thank you, papaji. I appreciate your kind words. I'm still getting accustomed to everything, but I'm trying my best to settle in.

Mr. Shah: That's good to hear. Remember, this is your home now, and we want you to feel like a part of the family. Your happiness is important for us.

Jaya: I understand, papaji. I'll do my best to contribute to the family's happiness. Thank you for your warm welcome.

Mr. Shah nodded, giving Jaya a promising smile before returning his attention to his dinner. It gave her reassurance that she was accepted and welcomed in the household. She hoped that with time, she would be able to build a close bond with him and the rest of the family.

Later that night Hitesh told Jaya that his mother was a little upset as Jaya did not cook dinner.

Hitesh: She should be fine by tomorrow so make sure not to do anything which makes her upset.

Jaya: Hitesh, I understand and respect your mother's role in the family. I have no intention of disregarding her authority or decisions. I am willing to listen to her and follow her guidance. I just hope that with time, we can develop a better understanding.

Hitesh: That's good to hear, Jaya. I believe that as you spend more time with mom, you'll come to see the love and care she has for all of us. She can be strict at times, but she is concerned a lot for us. I hope you'll be patient and understand her intentions soon.

Jaya: Of course, Hitesh. I will be patient and understanding. Family dynamics can take time to adjust and I'm committed to building a harmonious relationship with your mother. I want her to see me as a daughter and feel my respect for her.

Hitesh smiled at Jaya, appreciating her willingness to embrace the family bonds. He knew it wouldn't be an easy journey, but he believed that their love and understanding for each other would help them overcome any challenges that may arise. They both hoped for a positive and nurturing environment where everyone could thrive and support one another.

It took Jaya a few days to understand the rules and regulations. She observed that Snehlata doesn't like Jaya much, and Hitesh was always busy in his business and Nisha busy in her studies.

Jaya's daily routine became monotonous and suffocating as she tried to adapt to Snehlata's strict rule book which seemed to dictate every aspect, of their daily lives, from sleep schedules to meal plans, leaving Jaya feeling trapped and restricted. The absence of open communication with Hitesh added to her frustration, as he appeared to mirror his father's stoic nature.

Snehlata's constant rudeness and snide remarks further isolated Jaya, making it challenging for her to connect with her mother-in-law. She couldn't understand why her mother-in-law had such a negative attitude towards her and her family. Nisha, although kind and friendly, was busy with her studies, leaving Jaya longing for more companionship.

Feeling bored and lonely, Jaya found solace in her conversations with Dulari Kaki. The older woman became her confidante, someone she could share her joys and sorrows within the confines of their home.

One day, Nisha invited Jaya for a shopping outing. She instantly agreed as it was a rare opportunity to break free from the confines of the house. Jaya felt relaxed & was happy as she indulged in street food and enjoyed the shopping spree with Nisha. It was a much-needed escape from her isolated existence.

Excitedly, Jaya presented the items she had bought, to her husband. However, Hitesh's minimal response and lack of enthusiasm dampened her spirits. His reserved nature and limited conversations with her made Jaya feel even more suppressed in her loneliness.

As the days passed, Jaya yearned for a deeper connection with her husband and a more fulfilling and meaningful life within the household. She hoped for a change in the environment, where open communication, love, and understanding could blossom.

One day, Jaya asked Hitesh if she could go to see her parents, and he nodded his head in yes while working on his laptop.

Hitesh: Sure, but please ask mother when you can go. Let me know what she says. I will drop you.

The next day Jaya approached Snehlata.

Jaya: Mummy Ji, I wanted to talk to you about something. I would like to go and visit my parents for a few days. It has been a while since I last saw them, and I miss them dearly. May I please have your permission?

Snehlata (Looking up from her tasks): Why do you want to go now? We have so many things going on here, and there are responsibilities to fulfil. Can't you postpone your visit?

Jaya: I understand, But it has been a long time since I spent quality time with my family. It would mean a lot to me to see them & spend some time. Also, one of my friend is getting married. I promise to fulfil all my responsibilities when I return.

Dulari Kaki: Let her go, Sneha bibi she hasn't seen her parents since her marriage. Also, I am here to get the work done. Don't you get worried!

Snehlata (Sighs): Fine, if it means that much to you, you may go. But remember, family duties come first, and you need to be back in time to fulfil your obligations here.

Jaya: Thank you, mummy ji, I truly appreciate your understanding. I will make sure to be back on time and take care of my responsibilities. Your support means a lot to me.

Snehlata (Nods): Just make sure you don't cause any inconvenience to us.

Jaya: Ji mummy ji, Thank you again for granting me permission. I will make sure everything goes smooth during my absence.

With Snehlata's reluctant approval, Jaya felt a glimmer of hope as she anticipated the chance to reunite with her family and have some good time together.

Before leaving for her parents' house Jaya asked Hitesh.

Jaya: Hitesh, I've been thinking about my career and personal growth. I have a degree in finance, and I have always been passionate about pursuing a career in that field. I want to contribute to our household & wish to achieve something in my professional life.

Hitesh: But Jaya, we have everything we need. I am taking care of the finances, and you are here to manage the household. There's no need for you to work and add unnecessary stress in your life.

Jaya: I understand that we are financially stable, Hitesh. But it's not just about the money. It's about my personal growth, utilizing my skills and education, and contributing to society in a meaningful way. It is important for me to have some purpose, fulfillment & independence. Its not only about financial aspect.

Hitesh: I appreciate your aspirations, Jaya. But right now, our priority is to maintain a harmonious and balanced household. You are supposed to take care of our home and family, which is a significant responsibility. Let's focus on that for now, and we can revisit the idea of your career in the future if the circumstances allow it.

The discussion between Jaya and Hitesh escalated into a heated argument, with both of them expressing their frustrations and grievances. The pent-up emotions for months of silent dissatisfaction came pouring out, and the atmosphere in the room grew tense.

Jaya felt disappointed by Hitesh's response. She was expecting a better support and understanding from her husband. However, she understood the necessities of their household and the importance of maintaining peace and stability. She decided to silently explore her career options and find ways to pursue her passion without compromising the harmony of their family.

Next day morning, Jaya was suprised to see her father sitting in the living room, which brought great joy & comfort for Jaya. As she was missing her parents & this event made her happy. She prepared tea & snacks for her father.

Snehlata, seated beside Jaya's father, glanced at him with a mix of curiosity and suspicion.

Snehlata: How come you are here, Sharma ji?

Sharma ji: We all were missing Jaya, so I decided to pay a visit. (Maintaining his composure, responded politely.)

Snehlata's tone carried a hint of defensiveness.

Snehlata: Why don't you trust us? Do you think we are incapable of keeping her happy?

Sharma ji quickly reassured Snehlata, understanding her concerns.

Sharma ji: No, no, Snehlata ji. That's not what I meant. I know that Jaya is happy here. But as her father, I simply wish to take her home for a few days. Also, Jaya's friend is getting married next week, and she asked if I could bring her to attend the wedding.

Snehlata: Alright, send her back on Tuesday then.

Sharma ji nodded in agreement, appreciating Snehlata's consent.

Sharma ji: Thank you, Snehlata ji. It would be wonderful if Hitesh ji could join us for the wedding, only if he is available.

Snehlata considered the request, contemplating Hitesh's availability.

Snehlata: I will discuss it with Hitesh. If he is free, he can go. Otherwise, we can arrange for a driver to bring Jaya back.

Sharma ji, with mixed feeling of releif & a little conern, watched as Snehlata left the room. He knew that Snehlata's response was not welcoming, but he was glad that she agreed to let Jaya come with him for a few days. He understood Snehlata's protective nature towards her daughter-in-law, but he also knew the importance of Jaya spending time with her family.

During her visit with her family, Jaya cherished every moment and immersed herself in their love and care. Her parents, sensing something amiss, gently probed her about her life at her in-laws' place.

Jaya's father, concerned for her well-being, asked with a hint of worry.

Sharma ji: Jaya, is everything alright at your in-laws' place? You can tell us if there's any problem.

Jaya, not wanting to burden her parents with her troubles and being a responsible daughter, reassured them with a smile.

Jaya: Don't worry Papa, my mother-in-law is straight forward & blunt in her talks. But overall, she is a good person, and I am happy there. Also, Nisha is like a little sister to me. We share a great bond.

Jaya's parents nodded, seemingly satisfied with her response. They trusted her judgment and respected her decision to maintain a positive outlook on her married life. However, they couldn't shake off their concerns completely, but they chose to support their daughter and her choices.

As the days passed, Jaya immersed herself in the warmth of her family and cherished the love and support she received from her parents and siblings.

Jaya knew that her visit would soon come to an end, and she would have to return to her in-laws' house, where new challenges and revelations awaited her.

Monday morning, on the day of Jaya's friend's wedding, she woke up feeling dizzy and weak. As the day progressed, her condition worsened, and she fainted before she could leave for her friend's house. Her family rushed her to the hospital, and they informed her in-laws about the situation.

To their disappointment, none of Jaya's in-laws were able to make it to the hospital except Nisha. Nisha, trying to provide an explanation, shared that her father and brother were scheduled to travel out of town for a business meeting, while her mother had a prior commitment at a charity event. However, Jaya's parents couldn't measure how her in-laws could let their daughter-in-law's health be overshadowed by other engagements. It was evident to them that Jaya was enduring significant pain and neglect in her marital home.

Anxiety-filled moments passed as Jaya's parents awaited the doctor's report. When the doctor returned with a bunch of reports in her hands, their hearts raced with anticipation.

Doctor: Don't worry, Jaya is perfectly fine. In fact, she has wonderful news. She's expecting a baby.

Jaya's parents were overjoyed to hear this unexpected revelation. The news of their daughter's pregnancy filled the atmosphere with happiness & joy. They realized that Jaya needed the utmost care and support, especially during this crucial phase of her life.

The challenges that lay ahead seemed discouraging, but their love and determination to protect Jaya and her unborn child grew stronger than ever.

Nisha informed her parents and Hitesh about Jaya's condition and requested that she can be allowed to accompany Jaya to the hospital.

After one day of observation in hospital Jaya was discharged and Nisha requested Jaya's parents to send Jaya with her to their home. Sensing the urgency of the situation, Jaya's parents agreed to let her go with Nisha. Before they left, Jaya's mother made a heartfelt request to Nisha.

Jaya's mother: Nisha, Jaya always speaks high about you. You must know how things are for her there. Please take care of her and her child.

Nisha reassured Jaya's mother with a warm smile and comforting words.

Nisha: Don't worry, Aunty. Jaya Bhabhi will be happy and well taken care of. I assure you this & please feel free to call or visit her anytime.

With those words, they all departed from the hospital. Nisha requested Hitesh to cancel his plans and stay at home to support Jaya. Although Hitesh complied, but the homecoming for Jaya lacked warmth and excitement. Her news was met with casual acceptance, as if an ordinary guest was expected. Only Nisha and Dulari Kaki showed genuine enthusiasm upon hearing the good news. Nisha guided Jaya to her room to rest, and later, Hitesh came to check on her.

Jaya: Congratulations, Hitesh. You're going to be a father.

Hitesh: Thanks, Jaya. Though I wasn't ready for a baby yet, it's okay.

Jaya: Why aren't you happy?

Hitesh (Opening his laptop): Of course, I'm happy. But right now, I'm focused on business and won't have much time for baby. You, Mom, Nisha, and Kaki will take care of our boy.

Jaya: How do you know it's a boy? It's too early to tell.

Hitesh: It's a family history. The first-born child in our family has always been a boy. By the way, drop the idea of working. Just focus on raising the kids and taking care of the family.

Jaya (Upset): You're making decisions without considering my wishes.

Hitesh: I know what's best for our family. Trust me.

Jaya felt heartbroken by Hitesh's lack of support. Snehlata continued to be indifferent towards her, adding more work and responsibilities to her plate. Jaya struggled to take care of her health, often relying on Nisha or the driver for doctor appointments. In the third month, Snehlata called Jaya and instructed her to call her parents.

Jaya was curious about the reason behind it.

Snehlata: It's a family custom. After the third month, the girl's parents should take her home, care for her and the baby. After a month, she returns with gifts for the family. We'll have a small feast and announce the good news.

Jaya expressed her disagreement with the ritual and refused to call her parents, which angered Snehlata. When Hitesh and his father returned home, Snehlata informed them about Jaya's refusal. They were unhappy with her defiance, and the next morning, Jaya was sent back to her parents' home.

This time, Jaya opened up to her parents and revealed the misery she had been enduring. They were shocked and unsure how to react. However, they assured her that they would do everything in their power to rectify the situation and asked her to forget about her troubles while she was with them. Jaya's mental and physical health had deteriorated, leading to multiple hospitalizations. The doctor emphasized the importance of stress-free living for the well-being of both Jaya and her child.

During the month spent with her parents, no one from Hitesh's family reached out or visited except for Nisha, who used to call her from her hostel. Nisha explained that she couldn't visit due to her exams. As the month came to an end, no one from Hitesh's family came to take Jaya back. Feeling neglected and abandoned, Jaya decided to extend her stay with her family.

Two months later, Hitesh called Jaya's father and expressed his desire to bring her back. Jaya's father agreed and requested that he should personally come and retrieve her.

When Hitesh arrived to take Jaya back, despite Jaya's reluctance, her father sent a lot of gifts for the entire family as a good gesture. Jaya hoped that this act and the two months of separation would have brought some positive change in Hitesh and the overall atmosphere at her in-laws' home. However, to her disappointment, nothing seemed to have changed. Hitesh remained indifferent, his mother continued with her hurtful comments, and Mr. Shah remained silent as always.

Jaya tried to convince herself that once the baby is born, things should change. She held onto the hope that her life would become busy and focused on caring her child. This became the sole source of excitement left in her life amidst the ongoing challenges and disappointments.

One day, after having breakfast, Jaya suddenly experienced severe stomach pain, rendering her unable to walk. In distress, she called out to Snehlata for help. Snehlata immediately called for an ambulance. Jaya pleaded with Snehlata to let her go to the doctor with the driver, but Snehlata insisted on waiting for the ambulance, citing safety concerns. The pain was excruciating, and unfortunately, it took 30 minutes for the ambulance to arrive and another 30 minutes to reach the hospital.

Jaya lost consciousness and was rushed to the emergency room. Upon hearing the news, Hitesh and Jaya's parents arrived at the hospital. Jaya's condition remained unstable, and she remained unconscious in the ICU for two days. When she finally regained consciousness, she saw her parents, in-laws, and Hitesh gathered around her. She felt a bit of lightness in her body but couldn't comprehend what had happened. Then, she touched her belly and realized it was empty. She looked at her mother-in-law and asked what had happened. No one spoke a word. Overwhelmed with pain and exhaustion, Jaya screamed. The nurse came and tried to console her, explaining that due to her unstable condition, an emergency operation had been performed. Unfortunately, the baby could not be saved.

Jaya was shattered, losing her last hope of her life. She cried throughout the night, consumed with grief. The doctors informed Hitesh and Jaya's parents that her health was fragile and she couldn't bear any more stress. They advised against planning another pregnancy for at least the next year and a half, emphasizing the need for rest and care.

Nisha was called from college and asked to stay by Jaya's side in the hospital for few days. Jaya's parents were there, offering their support. Her in-laws and Hitesh visited her on alternate days. After few days, the doctor discharged Jaya, emphasizing the importance of proper care.

However, when Jaya was discharged, Hitesh didn't come to receive her. He simply called her father and suggested that she would feel better and receive better care at her parents' home. Her father agreed and took her back home. It took Jaya two months to recover physically, during which she received only a few formal calls from Hitesh and occasional visits from Nisha.

After two months, Jaya returned to her in-laws' place, but this time she went alone. She gathered her belongings, placed divorce papers on Hitesh's study table, bid farewell to Nisha and Dulari kaki, and left with a heavy heart. Her parents supported her decision, and after a series of hearings and arguments, she finally obtained a divorce from Hitesh.

Following the incident, Jaya requested to live independently, and her parents respected her decision, though they wanted her to stay with them. After enduring this struggle, Jaya faced new challenges in the following years. Today, she works as a CFO in a reputable government bank. Jaya chose not to remarry and instead adopted a baby girl, dedicating herself to raising her. Her siblings were inspired by her resilience and success, flourishing in their own careers.

As Jaya reflects on her past, she sees the hollowness and pain that once consumed her. The loss of her baby shattered her, but it also fuelled her determination to fight against all odds. She has become an inspiration to many other 'Jayas' who face similar circumstances.

KITTU

Love knows no boundaries for both humans and animals. The capacity of love is universal and can be experienced and expressed by all beings.

One fine day, as a daily routine, my mom went to feed the neighbour's cows. On the way, crossing our mango orchard, she found a kitten howling. She stopped for a while and tried to find the kitten's mother but couldn't find. She gave a small piece of chapatti to the kitten and went to feed the cow. While returning, she found the kitten still sitting there.

The same events happened on the following days as well. On the fourth day, she intentionally carried one chapatti for the kitten. By that time, he had also got familiar with my mom's routine. One day, he followed mom while she was returning home. However, due to some superstitions, he was forced to go back to the orchards.

Due to the lack of awareness regarding his potential rejection, the kitten continued to visit our home every day, using the back gate entrance.

His innocent face and sweet smile melted mine and my sister's hearts. After several days of effort, we finally managed to convince our family to nurture him but on the strict condition that he will not be allowed inside the house but only in the lawn outside.

Now, the big question was about the safety of the kitten whom we named 'Kittu' from our pet Dog "Dompy", a mischievous cross Pomeranian.

Slowly, Kittu started recognising his name and became familiar with everyone. He was provided with necessary accessories in the lawn itself and he discovered a safe place to sleep inside a shoe rack on the porch. He used to come late at night when no one could see him.

During winter days, whenever we would sit in the sun, Kittu would always find his way to my lap, sometimes even in my sister's lap. I have fond memories of him curling up and sleeping for hours. Even when my mother would be sitting on the carpet, he would silently approach her and sit beside her. Despite her attempts to shoo him away, he would stubbornly expect her to cuddle him, which always brought laughter to our hearts.

Upon my return from college, he would constantly hover around me, yearning to be held. He always craved attention. While eating, he would fix his gaze on me with his tender eyes, seemingly pleading for something.

I was constantly surrounded by children of a very young age throughout, till my postgraduation, which was unusual given the age gap between us. My father always found it peculiar and amusing that I would tell stories to those young kids or engage in play with them. However, Kittu was always delighted in these activities and eagerly joined our storytelling and playtime.

Kittu, having observed my father's lack of fondness for cats and kittens, instinctively kept a safe distance from him. While Kittu may not have won over my father completely, we noticed that he would often find amusement in watching our playful interactions with Kittu.

Dompy, on the other end, was quite hurt and full of anger after observing the diluted love and affection he received from the family members after Kittu's arrival. To add fuel to the fire, Kittu used to tease him by coming to the porch in the daytime and stealing his food. Tom and Jerry show started but this time it was between a dog and a cat.

One year passed and Kittu became part of our family.

One day, when I reached home, I saw Kittu injured. I inquired how it happened and came to know that not only humans, but animals too have rules to live. Kittu was a wild kitten and living so closely with humans was disliked by other wild cats. He didn't even had a mother to protect him as he was abandoned by her when he was only a few days old. The big, wild cats started harming him, and Kittu, being quite young, was incapable to fight with them. Kittu was attacked several times and even after medicines and home remedies, he was unable to recover. The jealousy and hatred of others were affecting him, and his health deteriorated day by day.

One day, he left home and didn't come back. We searched for him aggressively but could not find him. A few days later, Kittu was found dead in the woods. He was suffering from wounds and infections.

Tragically, it was not the physical wounds, but the mental scars and the pain inflicted by others that ultimately led to the kitten's demise.

Despite of spending short time together, the profound impact he had on my heart was immeasurable. His presence shattered any superstitious thoughts or beliefs I may have held about cats, replacing them with a deep appreciation and understanding of their worth.

Miss you, Kittu…

THE SLITHERING DESTINY

■ Early 1990s:

Jordan

A Little Kid with numerous dreams in his eyes, hopes in his heart and aspirations in his mind. He loved to go to school, enjoyed playing with friends and was emotionally attached to the place where he lived. While growing up, he used to hear his parents talking about a place where they belonged to.
So, this was not his motherland where he was born. His parents kept on talking about another land which was even more beautiful.

Despite a lot of struggles in life and questions in mind, a sense of fulfilment and satisfaction, hopes and dreams kept him engaged and motivated him along the way.

■ 2015

I met Feras:

I was in Bengaluru for my NGO work. I reached office in the morning and came across many new faces. I had met many of them in previous meets, however, one guy whom I haven't met before looked quite welcoming and striking. His features were sharp, and I could sense he was not an Indian.

I stepped ahead and greeted him.

With a smiling face, glowing eyes, and warm gestures, he said, 'Hi, Rita. How are you? I am Feras from Jordan. This is my first visit to India for this project. I heard that you are coming today for the meeting.'

He further asked me about my flight, job, and my stay in Bengaluru.

I was surprised with the way he was interacting. It was friendly and made me very comfortable. More than listening to his questions, I was observing his gestures and his approach which was worth appreciating. We started working on the same project and later he moved to Delhi to work on the same. We used to meet once a week for project discussions.

One fine day, I was reading about a country sharing borders with Jordan. The country was famous for historical places, natural beauty, holy places, and several other interesting activities but unfortunately suffered due to political issues, disturbed economy, war, etc. I asked Feras if he knows anything about this place as it was his neighbour country.

He smiled, listened patiently to whatever I asked and replied, 'I know everything about this place. Ask me what you want to know.'

I was perplexed and mockingly asked him if he is Google to know *everything*.

He then told me about his past. He stayed there for 7 years, it was his home country. He had to leave the country, his home, his relatives, and his friends as the conditions were becoming crumbling day by day.

He told me that he was born and brought up in Jordan but misses his home country a lot and wished to go back if the situation gets back to normal.

■ 1995
Homeland

A boy was in his ancestral home, a huge house with massive rooms. Everything there had layers of dust. He found a few old, black & white pictures lying on a rack. He then realized that this was the beautiful country which his parents used to talk about in Jordan. But now it was a new journey with ups and downs, however beautiful, in every manner. When your roots are connected to a place, then inevitably a feeling of belongingness arises.

■ 1997

FERAS: Life was moving on with struggles & hurdles. One Day while playing in a lawn with his friends, he suddenly heard his friends shouting, 'Run and hide!'

He turned around and saw big trucks packed with Soldiers coming towards them. Before he couldn't realise what was going on, his friends who were familiar with the situation dragged him inside a house. They asked him to sit there quietly. For the first time in his life, he witnessed such kind of dramatic incident. He hid himself in the corner of the bed because of impending danger.

At the age of 7, he was not able to figure out the situation. But soon he became familiar with such small hide-and-seek games between them and Army. Gradually, these instances became a part of his life and soon he got accustomed to such situations. Hearing bombardings & gun firings while returning home from school was not a strange thing and he became an expert in hiding and protecting himself.

Every day, his mother used to wait at home with tears in her eyes and praying to receive her kids safely back from school.

■ 2002

Years after he left his homeland, sitting in his home, he remembered those 7 years which he spent there with tears in his eyes.

His father had promised his grandfather that he will go back to his homeland once everything will be normal. He even fulfilled his promise, but once an unfortunate incident happened and he was forced to come back to Jordan leaving behind all memories.

What had happened?

Destiny forced them……

One noon, while coming back from school with his sisters and aunt, Feras was stopped by soldiers and was asked to go back. They were five kids, all under 11 years of age. Their home was in the opposite direction, but the soldiers' firm orders left them with no option & they were pushed back. After some time, the soldiers left, and the kids silently proceeded towards their home. They had a sense of relief that they were allowed to pass the security check and go home. By that time, it started drizzling.

After a few minutes' of walk, they heard a heavy, disturbing sound, they turned back and found a tanker approaching towards them. They were shocked and frozen with fear. They suddenly started running, knocked doors for help but didn't succeed. Drizzle had turned to heavy rain by then. Fully drenched in the rain, they were struggling with the heavy school bags. They stopped in front of a small building and knocked on the door hard, but all efforts failed and by that time the tanker was getting closer.

They even witnessed a cruel death in front of them. They all were shivering with fear. It was a dreadful moment. Feras recalled all the lovely moments he spent there and thanked God for the beautiful journey he had till date. He felt sorry for his parents for leaving them alone, and helpless for being unable to do anything for his sisters in that situation. He thought that his destiny is defined & that was the moment for him to leave the world.

After a while, they saw the tankers moving away and slowly fading from their visibility. They were all crying and were relieved to see themselves alive. It was a nightmare as everything was going to finish. For the first time, they felt a real terror, and later, these incidents continued in different ways.

Eventually, the fear of losing their lives outweighed the promise of staying in the motherland.

So, they decided to move back to Jordan.

A new life, new challenges, and new hope.

▪ 2015

After listening to these stories, I had a mixed reaction. I got goosebumps and could understand the connection Feras had with his homeland. It was really painful and sad. I felt pity for him for all the glitches he had gone through. I saluted his gestures, and the Positivity he brings to life.

While talking to FERAS I imagined a little kid in front of me and I asked a question, 'Why the hell you were going to school in such a situation?'

He replied, 'To live, to survive, to see my country free, to get a good higher education, a good job. Education was my weapon to live, survive and grow. I was not afraid of death. If Allah destined it for me, it would happen. But living without education and with fear, NO.'

He could not be native of that country as God has destined, but his attachment was deep & he grew up as a brave human fighting difficult life situations.

He saw people dying and getting killed in front of him. He saw the pain and fear of losing life.

What if he decided to leave school or if these incidents made a negative impact on his mind, he would have chosen the wrong path. Like many others, he would have ruined his life with other innocent lives connected to him. Fortunately, his deeds and dreams kept him positive and today he is living a far better life with dignity. Now he had achieved many dreams & was progressing towards brighter future.

We often read about war victims and jump to conclusions. We all are the same and nobody chooses to be a victim. It is the circumstances that are destroying lives, civilizations, nature, and peace of this beautiful world. Everyone is getting hurt and affected and none of the sides remains happy and with peace.

FERAS was one of the most charming people I ever met. He was a music lover, foodie, adventurous, and a happy face with so many horrible experiences hidden and locked within.

This story is dedicated to all those little Feras who lived their life under such horrible experiences yet successfully fought and overcame them against all odds.

ALPVIRAM

■ Kargil

It was dark all around, nothing but smoke and deafening noises of bullets & explosives. The noise was so terrifying that everyone's screams were drained out. The darkness was so deep that nothing was visible. The freezing snow was covered by the heat of the ammunition.

Suddenly, the smoke started to dissipate, noise subsided & the weather was turning colder. When Vishal tried to look through his blurred vision, he could see a wavering Tricolor flag being celebrated by few comrades.

Finally, they achieved victory over the enemies. He was elated to see that but also felt some heaviness in his chest.

As Vishal took a step forward, he stumbled & fell upon pile of dead bodies of Martyrs below.

He was horrified to see his mates dead. After a while, the chest pain subsided, bleeding stopped & he felt lighter.

He went closer to the martyr bodies & noticed that the smoke is even more dense, darkness was at peak, there were strong winds which was slowly carrying him away & gradually everything faded.

■ Dehradun

Seema, Seema!', say something, Seema.

Everyone pleaded Seema, desperately hoping for a response.

Voices filled with concerns, people called out to her repeatedly. 'Seema, please say something. Look around, & say something.

Family members, relatives & friends tried to break her silence. But Seema remained silent, her expression was cold with profound unease and uncertainty.

She stood motionless, her eyes fixed on Vishal's body, which was draped in the Tricolor, a symbol of sacrifice and honour.

She continued to stare her husbands' dead body. She was so stunned that her inner screams were suppressing the external noises & mournings.

Seema was tightly holding a document which looked like a medical report, which she received a day before.

Her mind raced with uncertainty that why Vishal left her with conflicting emotions. She was wondering with deep pain that if Vishal would ever see her expressions, would listen to her voice again & if he would ever come to know about most precious news that she was expecting their first child.

Their fate was shattered, she was completely broken & looking at her report she was perplexed if God has planned to fill the void & Vishal's soul will return in their child.

THE LAST DREAM

■ 20 November 2022

He went into a deep sleep with his soul penetrating the past with the experience of vivid dreams and memories from the earlier, as if his soul was retracing the footsteps of his childhood.

His thoughts went rolling back to the 1950s, where he saw himself as that curious and adventurous boy, running freely in the hills of Pauri Garhwal. The village of Nau Gaon, nestled atop the hill with its handful of families, was his world. He recalled the simple joys of his upbringing, playing with his siblings, and spending endless hours exploring the woods alongside the sheep and cows. Nature was his constant companion, and the beauty of the surroundings captivated his young heart. He was born there and grew up there till his teenage.

His father held a dual role as a *vaidh*, an ayurvedic doctor skilled in herbal remedies, and a priest, guiding the people of their community on the spiritual path. The boy found solace in the harmonious balance between the healing arts and the sacred rituals of their village.

With his siblings as the only companions, the boy embraced the wonders of nature that surrounded them. Together, they roamed freely through the woods, their laughter echoing in the serene landscapes. Their playful spirits intertwined with the sheep and cows, forming a harmonious connection with the animal kingdom. The vibrant wings of butterflies fluttered around them, tempting the boy's curiosity.

One fateful day his innocence led him to chase some bees thinking they were baby butterflies and reached the honeycomb. Unfortunately, the comb broke and the bees attacked him. He tried to run, but his small feet couldn't support him much and bees caught him in a couple of minutes. He was bitten by bees badly and he fainted, his brothers and sisters spotted him.

His unconscious state lasted for two days, during which his father, being a *vaidh* (ayurvedic doctor), applied herbal remedies and medicines to alleviate his pain. The remote location of their village made it difficult to seek immediate medical attention in the city.

In the midst of tension and gloom that shrouded their humble home, the family anxiously awaited a glimmer of hope. Two days passed with worry etched on their faces, their hearts heavy with concern. Yet, deep within the young boy's spirit, a strength resonated, urging him to persevere.

Life continued and days passed through thick and thins. As he approached the end of his primary school years, the absence of a secondary school in their village presented a challenge. Determined to continue his education, the young boy, accompanied by his brothers, enrolled in a school in a distant village. Despite the long and arduous journey, they persevered, driven by their thirst for knowledge and the desire for a better future.

Although separated from their village, the young boy understood the value of education and the doors it could open. He recognized that by pursuing his studies, he was not only shaping his own destiny but also uplifting his family and community.

After completing high school, the young boy stood at crossroads, eager to pursue higher education and broaden his horizons. Filled with dreams and aspirations, he approached his father, hoping for support and encouragement to continue his studies. Sadly, his father carried the weight of a heavy family burden, responsible not just for his own six children but also for his late brother's four young daughters. Tragically, his brother had passed away, leaving behind his daughters, who were now depended on them (his father) for care. In the face of this challenge, his father held a traditional perspective.

With a heavy heart, his father advised him against pursuing higher studies, emphasizing the need to prioritize the family's financial stability. He urged the young boy to join some job and contribute to the family's income instead.

Although disappointed by his father's response, the young boy understood the impor of his family's responsibilities. He recognized the sacrifices his father had made and the challenges they faced in their modest lifestyle.

However, deep within him, a fire burned, an unyielding determination to rise above his circumstances and create a better future for himself and his loved ones. With determination and resourcefulness, he sought alternative paths to continue his studies, driven by a deep belief in the transformative power of knowledge.

So, he left home and embarked on a journey of self-reliance. Despite the challenges of living alone and his short temper, he sought employment in various places, valuing the lessons and experiences that life had to offer. With each job, he saved diligently, slowly accumulating the funds necessary to pursue his education. His resilience and unwavering commitment led him to successfully complete his graduation, marking a significant milestone in his journey of personal and academic growth.

Despite the physical distance that separated him from his family, his love and affection for them remained unwavering. He made it a point to visit his family regularly, bridging the gap with his presence and nurturing the bonds that tied them together.

Despite his father's insistence and the availability of a secure government job at the post office, he made the bold decision to follow his own path. Refusing to settle for a comfortable yet unfulfilling career, he chose to pursue his passions and dreams instead. This decision left his father disappointed, his mother saddened, and his siblings perplexed, as they struggled to understand his unconventional choice. However, he remained steadfast in his determination to forge his own destiny, even if it meant facing uncertainty and challenges along the way.

Motivated by the hardships he witnessed in remote villages, where people struggled for basic necessities, he chose to return to the city. With a determined mindset, he delved into work, dedicating his entire time to his job, tirelessly working day in and day out. He even ventured into the forest, taking on a job that required him to stay in the wilderness for days at a time. Through his extensive travels across various cities, particularly in northern parts of India, he gained valuable experience and developed resilience, becoming a formidable individual.

He continued to financially support his family in the village, saving money diligently. The traditional mindset of his parents longed for everyone to stay together, even with limited means. His mother and father made several attempts to persuade him to return, but their efforts went in vain. Eventually, after a few years, his parents decided to arrange his marriage. As a new chapter in his life began, he embraced the change and found happiness in his marital union.

In his relentless pursuit of providing a better life for his family, he had to sacrifice his newly married life and departed for the work again. It was a decision driven by his unwavering commitment to the well-being of his loved ones. During his absence, his parents urged his wife to persuade him to return and reside with them. Conversely, he encouraged his wife to convince his parents to come and live with him. Eventually, after enduring long distances and discussions, his wife made the decision to join him and support him in his struggles. Together, they moved on with a new phase of life in a small rented apartment. He continued to work tirelessly, but the change was that now he received breakfast and dinner, he was thankful to his wife's presence and care.

After experiencing the joy of their first child, a daughter their happiness was overshadowed by the cruel hand of fate. Due to a medical condition, their precious angel was taken away from them. The pain they endured was unimaginable. Despite their immense grief, they found solace in each other's company and shared the burden of their losses. With limited emotional support, they decided to bring his parents to live with them. However, his parents, although pleased to witness his growth, were not prepared to permanently leave their hometown. They opted to stay for a while and then return to the comfort of their village.

After a year they were again blessed with a baby girl but, tragically, destiny once again dealt them with a cruel hand. Their happiness was short-lived. Unexpectedly, their baby girl's health took a turn for the worse, and despite their desperate efforts, she could not be saved.

Devastated by the loss of their second child, the couple was shattered. The weight of grief seemed unbearable, and they felt utterly alone. In the absence of family support during such a challenging time made the burden even heavier to bear.

With the passage of time, their fortunes began to turn. He achieved financial stability and successfully established his own business. His dedication and hard work paid off, allowing him to support his younger siblings and provide a comfortable life for his own growing family. The family was blessed with two baby girls and a boy, bringing immeasurable joy and fulfilment to their lives.

As their circumstances improved, he eagerly embarked on the journey of building his dream house—a place where he envisioned his parents, wife, and children living together in harmony. It was a symbol of his enduring love for his family and a testament to his determination to create a haven for his loved ones. Even though physical distances separated them, his frequent visits to his parents reminded him that no matter how far he ventured, his heart remained rooted in the warmth of his childhood home and the unconditional love of his parents.

21 November 1986

What a beautiful day it was! He arrived in his new house with his family.

He worked hard and achieved his dream of building a new house for his family. Despite the challenges and losses, he faced along the way, his love for his family remained steadfast. With the support of his wife, they created a loving and nurturing environment for their children. The house became a symbol of their resilience and the bonds they shared.

He selflessly devoted himself to the happiness and well-being of his loved ones, despite experiencing loss and facing challenges along the way. He worked tirelessly to provide a wonderful life for his children, ensuring they had happiness and comfort. However, he often found himself absent from precious moments of his children's lives due to his dedication to work. He was missing those moments mostly because he was working hard to create those moments. His wife, on the other hand, fulfilled both the roles of a mother and a father in his absence. She stood by his side through thick and thins going extramile to maintain relationships with their extended family, friends, and relatives. Although he couldn't always match her level of commitment, he recognized and appreciated her unwavering support throughout their journey, as she remained steadfast and never asked for anything in return.

Time ran so fast. He lived for his loved ones and has lost many people in the journey of life. Some parted their ways physically, some emotionally but nothing stopped him from chasing his dreams.

As he entered his twilight years, his health began to decline, but his wife's loving care and attention revived him time to time again. Eventually, he reached a point where he desired rest and tranquillity. He gradually passed on the responsibility of the family and his business to his son, allowing himself to spend more time on spirituality and his well-being. After enduring the hardships and challenges of 70 long years, he yearned to make up for the moments he had missed during his years of struggle.

In the present day, he found himself lost in his dreams. He could hear the voices of people around him, their cries and shouts, and the faint whispers and murmurs about his life and journey. These voices carried with them the echoes of his past, reminding him of the impact he had made and the trials he had overcome.

■ 21 November 2022

As he bid farewell to the house he had built with passion and love, he knew that he was also leaving behind his family, friends, and everything that had constituted his world. The sounds of screams and cries gradually faded away until they disappeared entirely. With his eyes closed forever, a profound silence settled. The dream had come to an end, and so had his journey.

"For My Beloved Father"

MY SCRIBBLE VOYAGE

▪ How it started:

I was fond of reading and writing since my school days. I used to write poems and stories with my limited world of imaginations. I remember the day when I inculcated this habit. One day my sister handed me a book named "Meet Yourself" written by Orison Swett Marden, an inspirational American author. She insisted me to read the book and assured that I would love it. Initially I was hesitant as I was already loaded with many school books. So I didn't wanted more but still I kept the book with me. One day I got a chance to open & read it, and finally ended reading it completely at a stretch.

I truly loved reading it & for several days I was thinking over the content of the book. The book included many thought provoking incidents & situations. Gradually, I inherited the habit of gathering & penning down my imaginations & thoughts. This was also influenced by my father's habit of reading newspapers and magazines, as well as my mother's devotion to holy books. So, I also began to explore those for more ideas and thoughts. Also, I requested my sister to bring me few more books, which she happily did. My reading habit was gaining pace & interest. I finished reading these books in no time. Being a literature student, she had lot of books as part of her syllabus which included Shakespeare, George Bernard Shaw and more. Though, I was a beginner in reading, I managed to read books which were above my standards. I just read them out of curiosity, determining my own perceptions and meanings. Gradually my interest towards reading mushroomed.

■ **It continued:**

My parents, my biggest strengths were simple people with orthodox thinking. I enjoyed my reading and writing, and I was inventing my own world. However, it didn't excite my parents as they wanted me to focus more on academics and less on my hobbies. I did not blame them because as parents, they had their own concerns and care. During those times, pursuits like writing and creative endeavours were often regarded merely as hobbies rather than viable professions.

At that young age, I continued my interest in reading & writing even though words were limited in my dictionary. I kept my habit of story writing as a secret and even my close friends didn't have any clue about it.

■ **A phone call that changed my life:**

One day, I got a phone call from my classmate with shocking news. She told me that our close school friend died in a road accident. At that moment, I could not react because of the shock. I was stunned & didnt know how to react, I started weeping. At that age, when we were learning the meaning of life, I learnt the truth of death. I shuddered with no words to express. I coudn't sleep that night & till next morning I was mourning thinking about this tragic incident.

After a week, I gathered some courage and visited family of my deceased friend. I had no clue what will I talk to them, how to console or behave in front of them. However, I visited & shared the pain with them. After that incident, I was a changed person. I limited my friend circle, spoke to limited people and about things which were necessary and tried to focus on my studies and upcoming exams.

I saw two different worlds. At one end I was petrified with this incident, and on the other end, everything was normal. His close friends, other classmates were behaving normal. No one talked about him. It seemed that no one misses him. I wanted to talk about him with people and I wanted to tell everyone about my feelings. He was my partner in Hindi lectures but now I had an empty seat next to me. I used to bunk my math classes with him. I was crushed within, shattered completely and loneliness grew all over my little world. I picked up my pen and started writing again.

For the first time in my life, I wrote a real-life story, a narrative that has remained hidden within me, undisclosed to anyone so far.

■ A change in my style:

Gradually, I could sense some improvement in my writing skills. Before I used to imagine and write, but later I wrote about real incidents and personal experiences. I realized that it is easy to imagine a wonder world, write about it, make films, and fascinate people. Writing about a real-life story is challenging. To explain and make people understand the pain and to express ones' emotion is an uphill task.

I started to observe people, their life, emotions, behaviors & personalities.

I even got a chance to write articles for a few magazines and NGOs. I even created blogs multiple times but deleted all of them because of conflicts between my own thoughts.

■ Life goes on:

I successfully completed my studies, embarked on a fulfilling career, and found happiness in my marriage. Alongside these milestones, my passion for writing continued to thrive, thanks to two important individuals who have been pillars of support throughout my journey.

The first person who holds a special place in my heart is my sister, Sangita. It was her who discovered my hidden ability for storytelling and guided me towards this creative path. Her unwavering support and belief in my abilities have been instrumental in my growth as a writer.

The second is my life partner, who not only holds the esteemed role of being my spouse but also acts as the primary reader of all my stories. His & my sisters' unbiased feedback and encouragement have been invaluable in shaping my writing.

With my loving complete family and two adorable baby boys adding joy to my life, I am surrounded by love and motivation to continue honing my writing skills. I am grateful for the connections I have forged with these significant individuals and the influence they have had on my creative pursuits.

As I continue to write and embark on new literary adventures, I carry the love and support of these two individuals with me. They are the driving force behind my creativity, and their presence in my life is a constant reminder of the impact that art and storytelling can have.

With gratitude in my heart, I dedicate *My Story* to my sister Sangita, the person who has been by my side through it all. May our bond and shared love for literature continue to inspire and shape our journeys.

About The Author

Reeta was born in the magnificent lap of the Himalayas, into a Hindu Brahmin family. Her childhood was spent in the serene valley of Dehradun and its surrounding areas. From a young age, she has been a determined girl, nurturing lofty aspirations, believing in the power of dreams, and striving to achieve her life goals. Reeta's bond with her family, especially her parents, is strong and unyielding. Life has presented her with various challenges, but she has grown to become an emotional yet fearless individual.

With a postgraduate degree in Business Management and professional experience as an Operations Consultant, she has

About The Author

gained a diverse range of skills and knowledge. Alongside her professional pursuits, she finds immense joy in immersing herself in the world of books, satisfying her wanderlust through travel, and expressing her creativity through writing, painting, and other artistic endeavours.

She has a deep affinity for engaging in conversations, whether it be with familiar faces or strangers, as she finds great value in the emotional connections that lie beneath the surface. She firmly holds the belief that every individual carries within them a distinctive and captivating story, waiting to be discovered and shared.

Currently, she is settled in the United Arab Emirates with her small and loving family, comprising her husband and two young boys.

Made in the USA
Monee, IL
03 May 2026

49438944R00085